JENIFER DICK and ANGELA WALTERS
NINE-PATCH
Revolution
20 Modern Quilt Projects
stashBOOKS.
an imprint of C&T Publishing

PUBLISHER: Amy Marson

CREATIVE DIRECTOR: Gailen Runge

EDITORS: Liz Aneloski and Katie Van Amburg

TECHNICAL EDITOR: Linda Johnson

COVER/BOOK DESIGNER: April Mostek

PRODUCTION COORDINATOR: Tim Manibusan

PRODUCTION EDITOR: Alice Mace Nakanishi

ILLUSTRATORS: Linda Johnson and Kirstie L. Pettersen

STYLE PHOTOGRAPHY by Lucy Glover and **INSTRUCTIONAL PHOTOGRAPHY** by Mai Yong Vang of C&T Publishing, Inc., unless otherwise noted

Published by Stash Books, an imprint of C&T Publishing, Inc., P.O. Box 1456, Lafayette, CA 94549

Library of Congress Cataloging-in-Publication Data

Names: Dick, Jenifer, author. | Walters, Angela, 1979- author.

Title: Nine-patch revolution : 20 modern quilt projects / Jenifer Dick and Angela Walters.

Description: Lafayette, CA : Stash Books, an imprint of C&T Publishing, Inc., 2018.

Identifiers: LCCN 2017038391 | ISBN 9781617456022 (soft cover)

Subjects: LCSH: Patchwork--Patterns. | Quilting--Patterns. | Nine patch quilts.

Classification: LCC TT835 .D49 2018 | DDC 746.46/041--dc23

LC record available at https://lccn.loc.gov/2017038391

Printed in the USA

10 9 8 7 6 5 4 3 2

Dedication

FROM JENIFER
For Ray

FROM ANGELA
To Grandpa Ford, who taught me a love of quilting and Nine-Patch quilts

Acknowledgments

FROM JENIFER To Angela, thank you for joining me on this Nine-Patch journey! Your support and, of course, your beautiful quilting are continual sources of inspiration to me!

To the staff at C&T Publishing / Stash Books, and especially my editor, Liz—thank you for guiding me through the process with patience and kindness!

And to my wonderful family—thank you for supporting me as I wrote this book, even though it meant long hours in the sewing room and on the computer! I love you!

FROM ANGELA A big heartfelt thanks to Jenifer for dealing with me during this fun process. Big hugs to Liz, Amy, and the rest of the folks at C&T Publishing for always treating me like one of the family.

Contents

THE QUILTS

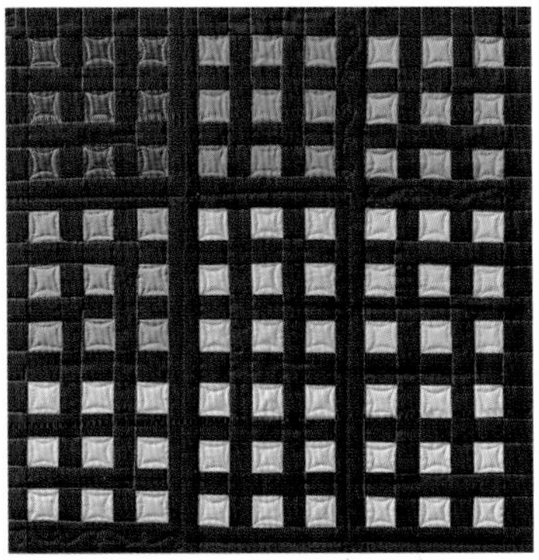

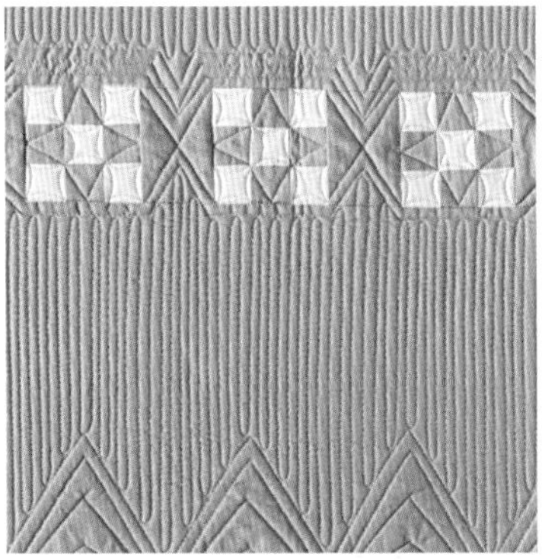

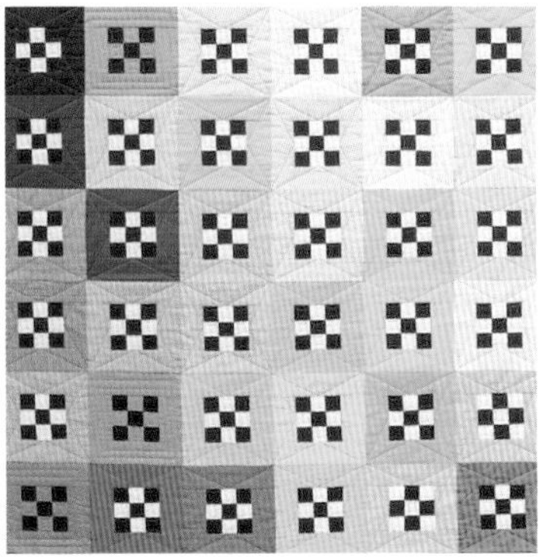

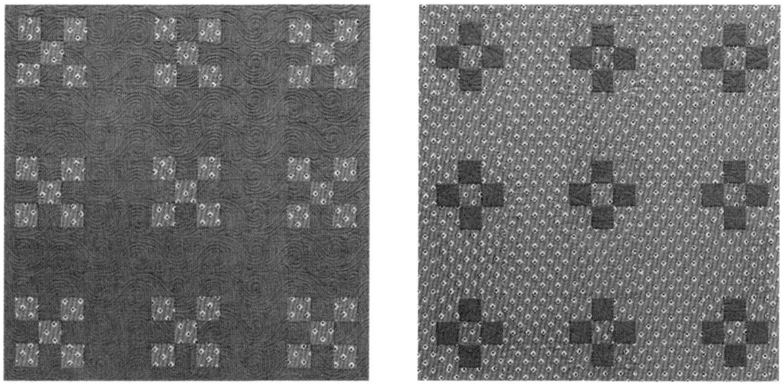

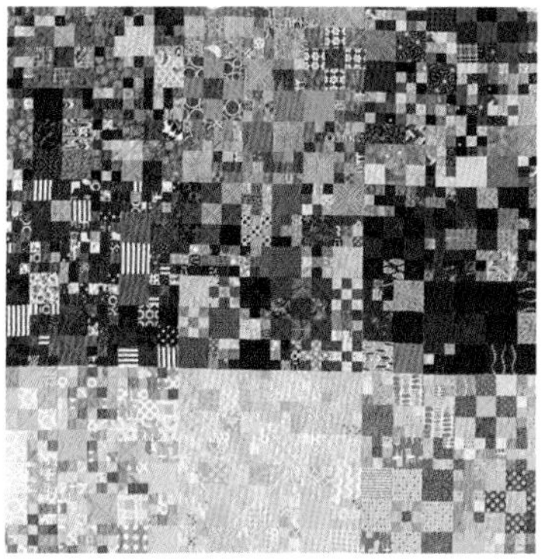

FOREWORD

Thoughts on a Nine-Patch Block

The quilts in this book are designed for both beginning quilters and more experienced quilters who are looking for quick, fun, and easy quilts! Whatever your skill level, you'll find something you want to make!

From Jenifer

Years ago the Nine-Patch—or rather one of its many, many variations—was my first quilt. From that initial introduction to the Nine-Patch block, I learned almost everything I needed to know about quiltmaking. But more importantly, through the process of making that humble Nine-Patch, I learned a fundamental truth about myself: I wanted to make more!

When Angela and I decided to write this book together, we knew that Nine-Patch–based quilts were the perfect avenue to teach a new generation of quilters. This both honors our personal beginnings and celebrates the future of the art we love so much!

I hope you enjoy the quilts in this book and find many ways to learn something new or just to relax and make something fun and charming! They are purposefully designed to not only pay tribute to the Nine-Patch but to bring a fresh, contemporary look to them as well.

Jenifer

From Angela

The Nine-Patch quilt block has a special place in my heart. When I learned how to quilt from my husband's grandfather, he patiently showed me how to make the Nine-Patch block. One block led to several, then to a finished quilt. The quilt was a gift to my husband, and to this day it is on our bed. I didn't grow up in a family of quilters, so I don't have treasured quilts from generations past. But I do have the legacy that Grandpa Ford gave me—a love for quilting. Whether the quilts you make from this book are your first or just your most recent, I hope that you enjoy the finished product as much as my husband and I do.

Happy quilting!

Angela

Basic Directions

Making a Nine-Patch Block

It's easy to see why the Nine-Patch block is so common with beginners and advanced stitchers alike: It's easy to piece, it's pleasing to look at, and it's versatile—the trifecta of quilt blocks!

The beauty of a Nine-Patch lies in its symmetry. Odd numbers tend to be appealing to the eye, so the natural proclivity of the Nine-Patch to be made of three rows of three units makes it inherently pleasing to look at.

Detail of *Three* (page 26)

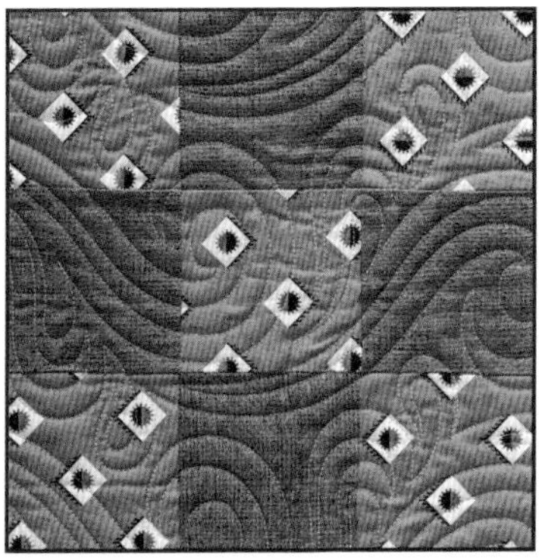

Detail of *Fraternal Twins* (page 70)

Detail of *The Importance of Being Pink* (page 110)

Piecing a Nine-Patch couldn't be any simpler. Sew a few straight seams and press them properly so they align perfectly, and you have a picture-perfect block! The blocks are easily scalable to almost any size and, in most cases, they play well with other blocks.

Once you master Nine-Patch construction, you can branch out to its numerous variations. The Nine-Patch is one of the most versatile quilt blocks. You can add in half-square or quarter-square triangles, elongate the blocks, skew the blocks, experiment with color placement, mix up unit sizes, and so on.

There are two ways to make a Nine-Patch: through basic construction or using strip sets.

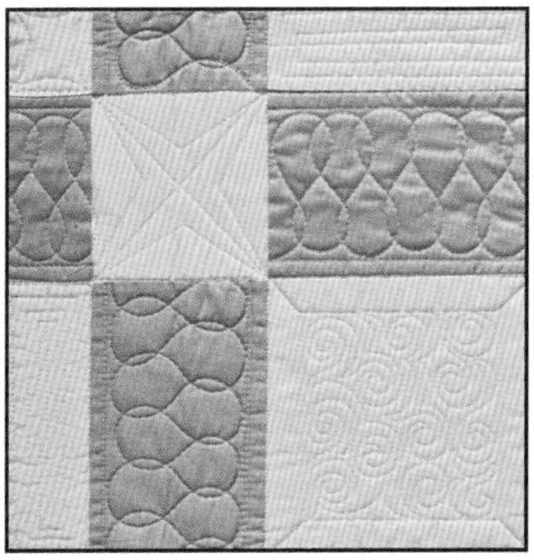

Detail of *Plaid* (page 87)

BASIC CONSTRUCTION

Basic construction is best to use when you only need a few Nine-Patches, or each block is different, or there are more than two fabrics in each block.

Start by knowing the size to cut the squares. The project will tell you, or you can use this chart if you know the finished size of the block.

Finished block size	Cut 9 squares per block.
3″ block	1½″ × 1½″
6″ block	2½″ × 2½″
9″ block	3½″ × 3½″
12″ block	4½″ × 4½″

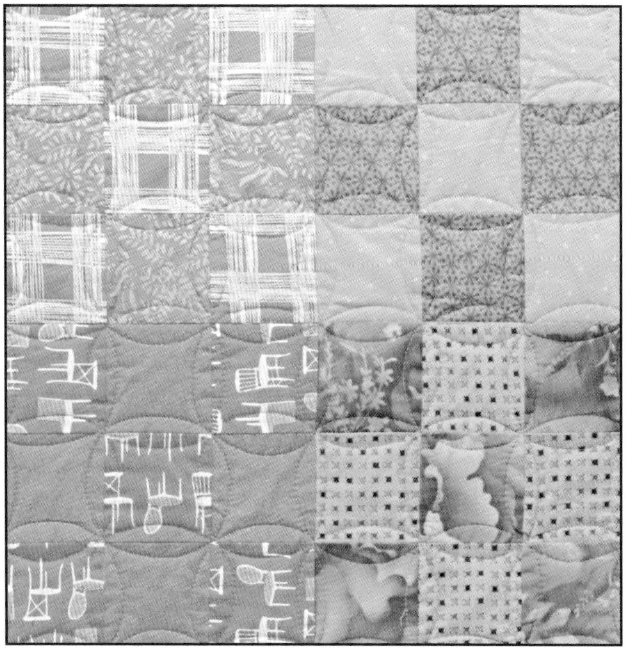

Detail of *Color Columns* (page 115). The blocks in this quilt are all unique with multiple fabrics. Basic construction is the easiest way to make the blocks.

Detail of *Stretch'd* (page 81). Only one Nine-Patch block is needed for this quilt, so basic construction is the best method to use.

Seam Allowances

A ¼″ seam allowance is used throughout this book. It's a good idea to do a test seam before you begin sewing to check that your ¼″ is accurate. Accuracy is the key to successful piecing.

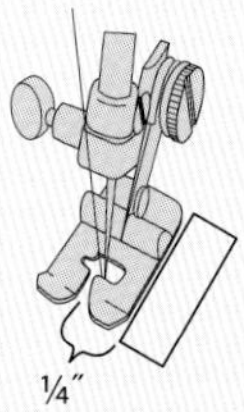

To test your seam allowance, cut 2 fabrics 2½″ × 2½″. Sew them together. Measure the sewn unit; it should measure 4½″ × 2½″. If it doesn't, make adjustments to the width of the seam allowance and repeat the test.

Once you have an accurate ¼″ seam allowance, you're good to sew!

Basic Construction: Making a 3″ Nine-Patch Block

STEP 1 Cut 9 squares 1½″ × 1½″.

STEP 2 Lay out the squares in 3 rows of 3 squares in the order you want them pieced. *Fig. A*

STEP 3 Sew the squares together into rows. Press. (To determine how to press the block, refer to Pressing, page 9.) *Fig. B*

STEP 4 Sew the rows together. Press. *Fig. C*

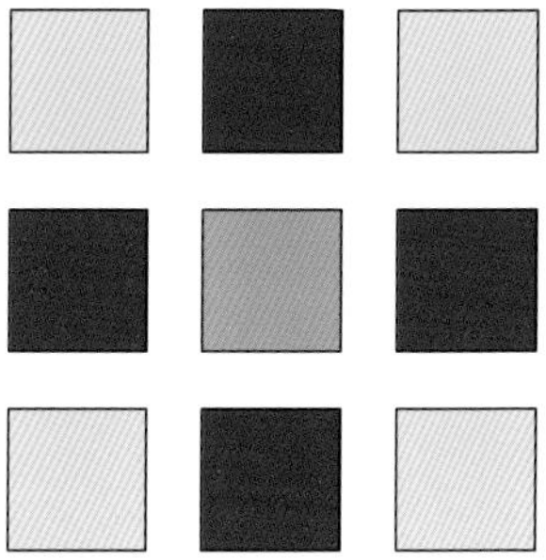

A

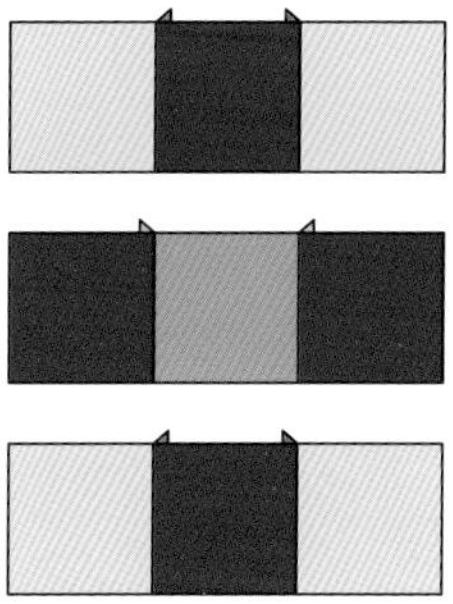

B

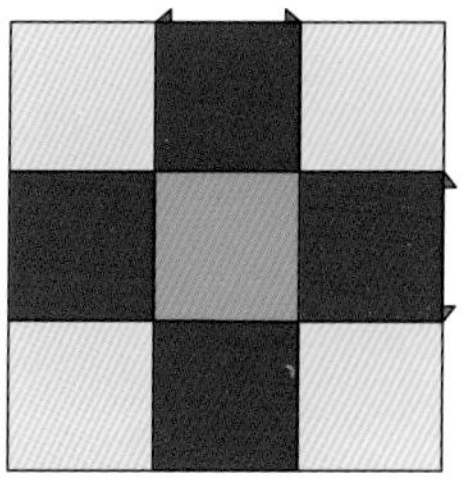

C 3″ Nine-Patch block made with basic construction

Pressing

Pressing Toward Darker Fabric

Pressing depends on how you use the block in the quilt. Most often, Nine-Patch seam allowances are pressed toward the darker fabric to keep it from showing through the light fabric in the finished quilt.

Detail of *Nine-Patch Surround* (page 61). The units are pressed to the dark gray, so the seam allowance doesn't show through the white units.

Pressing Open

Sometimes it's best to press for construction, meaning that in order to fit in with other blocks when completing the top, you might need to press differently. When fitting together many Nine-Patches, the easiest way to make sure the seams line up is to press the seams open.

Detail of *Controlled Chaos* (page 54). This is another multicolor scrappy quilt that is a good candidate for pressing the seams open. Because these blocks were sewn over time, not all at once, it would have been difficult to remember how to press. Pressing them open makes the process easier.

Pressing the seams open ensures a foolproof way to join multiple Nine-Patch blocks perfectly. This works best when the blocks are not identical or are multicolored, with no clear light and dark.

STEP 1 Press the seams open as you join each unit in the row. *Fig. A*

STEP 2 Press the seams open when you join the rows. *Fig. B*

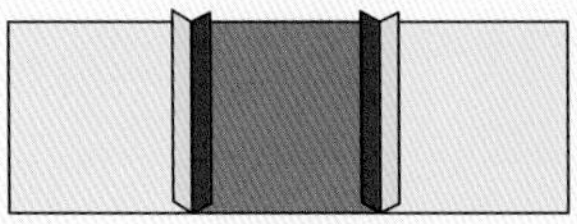

A

B

> NOTE
>
> If you press the seams open, never quilt-in-the-ditch. The quilting stitches will act like a saw and open up those seams. Also, choose bonded batting, so it won't beard or migrate through the seams to the top of the finished quilt.

Detail of *Medallion* (page 121). The seams in this quilt were all pressed open. Because the blocks are all different, it would be difficult to figure out how to press the seams so that they nest. Pressing seams open ensures they will all fit together without twisting or having to press again when setting together the blocks.

Pressing Seams in One Direction

Another option is to press the seams all in the same direction. This is best to use when all the blocks are identical; this ensures the seams nest properly when joining the blocks.

Pressing seams in one direction regardless of light and dark fabrics allows multiple blocks to fit together easily without flipped seams. Rotate the blocks when setting them together to nest together the seams. This works best when all the blocks are symmetrical and there is no up or down.

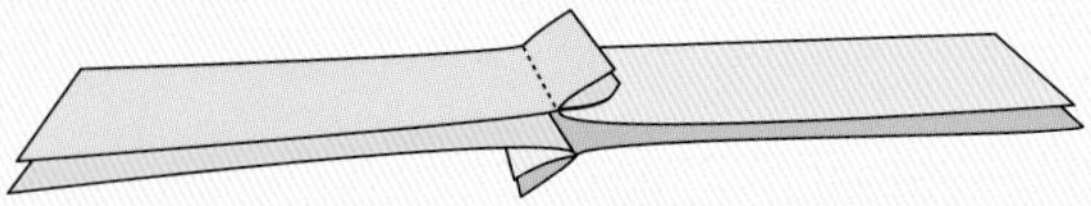

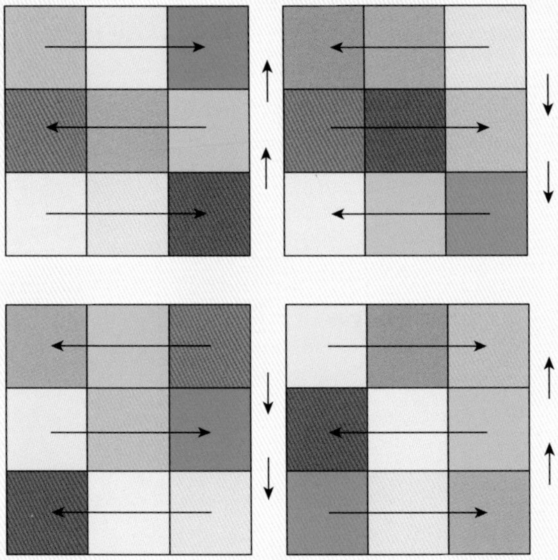

Arrows show how to press four blocks so they fit together with opposing seams and nest together when joining

STRIP-SET CONSTRUCTION

Strip-set construction is the fastest way to make Nine-Patches when the quilt calls for multiple, identical blocks. By piecing together long strips, then cutting the strips into units, you can achieve accurate piecing in less time than it takes to make multiple, identical blocks using basic construction.

Start by knowing the size to cut the strips. The project will tell you, or you can use this chart if you know the finished size of the block.

Finished block size	Cut strip size
3″ block	1½″ × WOF*
6″ block	2½″ × WOF
9″ block	3½″ × WOF
12″ block	4½″ × WOF

** WOF = width of fabric*

Detail of *Streaked Lightning* (page 65). All 28 Nine-Patch blocks in this quilt are identical, making strip piecing the fastest method.

Strip-Set Construction: Making a Batch of 3″ Nine-Patch Blocks

You will make a total of 28 identical Nine-Patch blocks.

STEP 1 From the darker fabric, cut 5 strips 1½″ × width of fabric. This fabric will show up on the 4 outer corners and in the center of the block.

STEP 2 From the lighter fabric, cut 4 strips 1½″ × width of fabric. This fabric will show up in the center of all 4 sides of the block.

STEP 3 Sew the fabrics together in long strips in the following configurations, and press the seams toward the dark. *Figs. A & B*

Unit 1: Light / dark / light. Make 1.

Unit 2: Dark / light / dark. Make 2.

STEP 4 Cut the sewn strips into units the same width that the original strips were cut; for this example, 1½″ wide. *Fig. C*

STEP 5 Sew Unit 1 to Unit 2. Add the second Unit 2. *Fig. D*

STEP 6 To press the block or to see alternate pressing ideas, refer to Pressing (page 9). *Fig. E*

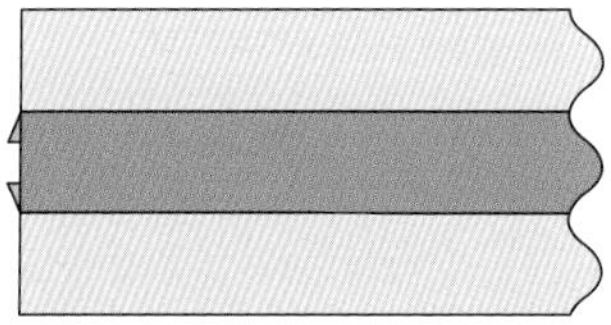

A Unit 1 strip set

B Unit 2 strip set

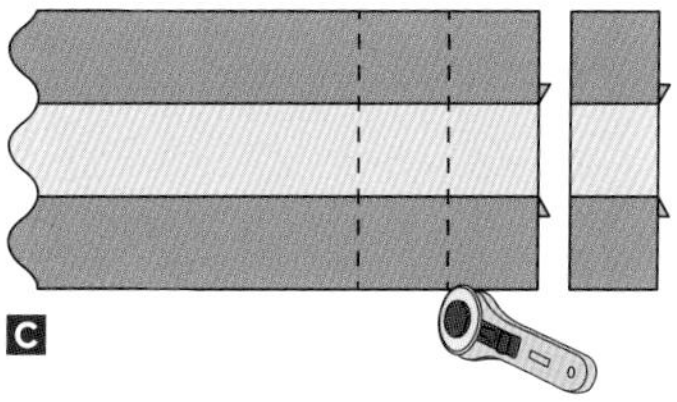

C

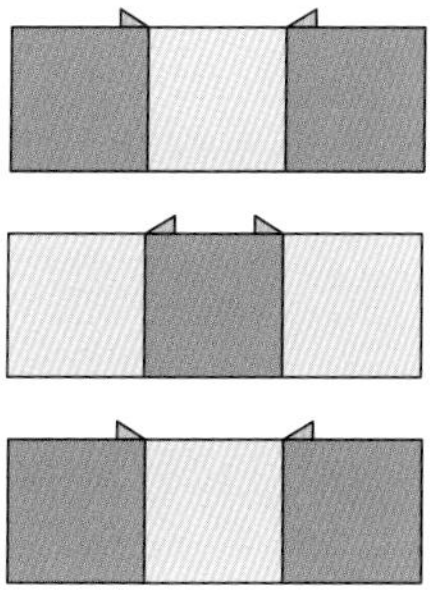

D

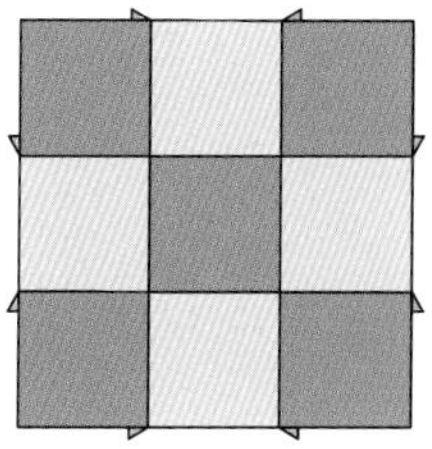

E 3″ Nine-Patch block made with strip-set construction

Finishing the Quilt

Once you complete the quilt top, you'll need to layer the top, batting, and backing into a quilt sandwich, then quilt and bind it. The following is an introduction to these concepts; follow your own favorite method for completion.

BORDERS

Many quilts in this book don't have borders. For those that do, it's important to measure through the center of the quilt top to find the correct cut lengths, so the borders don't end up wavy. Piece the borders as necessary to achieve the length needed. Pin to the edge and sew.

In most cases, you sew on the side borders first. When the quilt top is finished, measure it across the center vertically. This is the length to cut the side borders. Cut multiple strips and sew them together into 1 long strip to get the length needed. Place pins at the centers of all 4 sides of the quilt top, as well as in the center of each side border strip. Pin the side borders to the quilt top first, matching the center pins. Using a ¼″ seam allowance, sew the borders to the quilt top and press toward the border.

Measure horizontally across the center of the quilt top, including the side borders. This is the length to cut the top and bottom borders. Repeat the process you used for the side borders by pinning, sewing, and pressing.

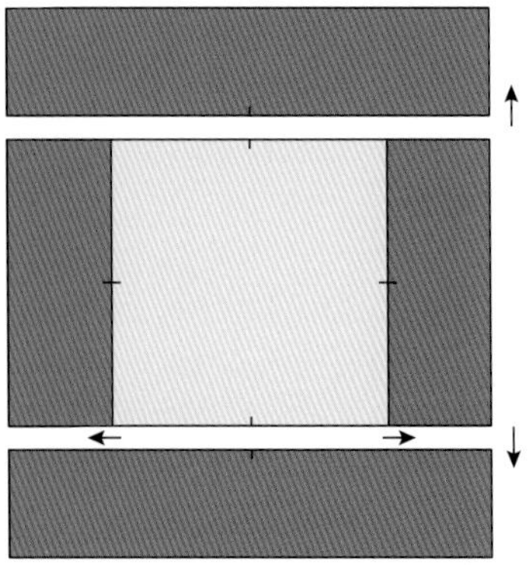

BACKING

The backing should be 4″–5″ larger on each side than the quilt top. Piece, when necessary, to make the backing large enough, or use a wide backing to avoid piecing altogether. The size needed is listed in each project. For smaller quilts this additional allowance can be adjusted to 3″–4″.

BATTING

The type of batting you choose is a personal preference. You'll want to consider the purpose of the quilt when making this decision. The size needed is listed in each project.

LAYERING AND BASTING

Spread the backing out, right side down, on a flat surface. Tape or pin it securely in place. Place the batting on top, smoothing out any wrinkles. Place the quilt top, right side up, on top, smoothing it out. Baste together the 3 layers (for machine quilting, baste pins spaced about 4″ apart; for hand quilting, thread basting works well).

QUILTING

In each quilt project, Angela provides detailed ideas, tips, and hints on how she quilted it. This is useful for the beginner—or anyone who has trouble deciding which quilting designs to use!

Quilting the Continuous Curve

You'll see many different quilting options in this book, including many fun variations of the continuous curve design.

Using continuous curve lines makes a fabulously versatile design perfect for Nine-Patch blocks. This handy design has been around a long time, and is worth learning since you can use it in so many different ways. You'll especially love that you can quilt the whole block without starting and stopping.

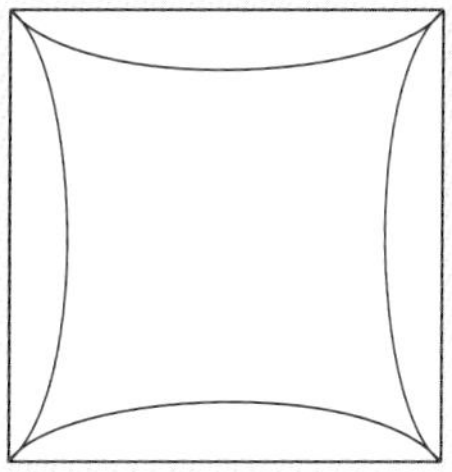

A

In One Square

The basic continuous curve design is a line that arcs to each corner of the block and then returns to the starting point. *Fig. A*

Don't worry too much about making the curves symmetrical; that will come with practice. Focus on trying to make the curves land as close to the corners as you can. Even if they aren't perfect, it will still look good.

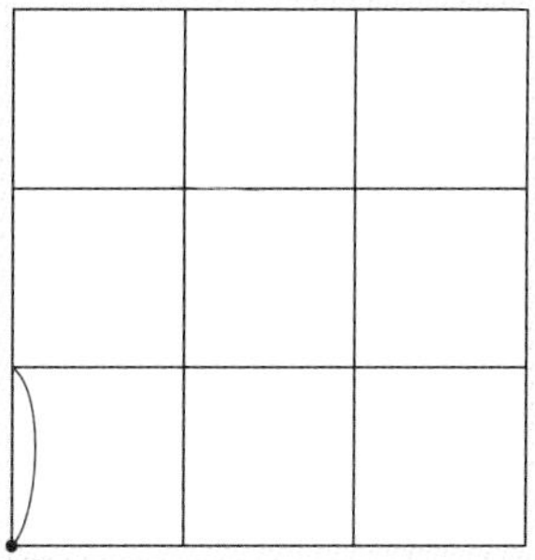

B

In Multiple Squares

Quilting the continuous curve in one square is fairly straightforward, but quilting blocks with multiple squares, like a Nine-Patch, requires a little more thought. You don't want to have to quilt each square separately; that would require traveling along the seams to reach them. The following method is far more efficient.

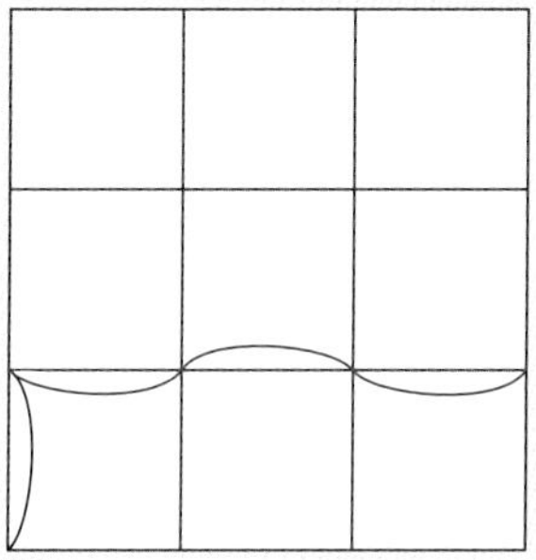

C

STEP 1 Starting from a corner, quilt a line that curves up to the point directly above it. *Fig. B*

STEP 2 Quilt a serpentine line that curves from point to point to the opposite side of the block. *Fig. C*

STEP 3 Return to the starting point in Step 2 by quilting a serpentine line that curves in the opposite direction. *Fig. D*

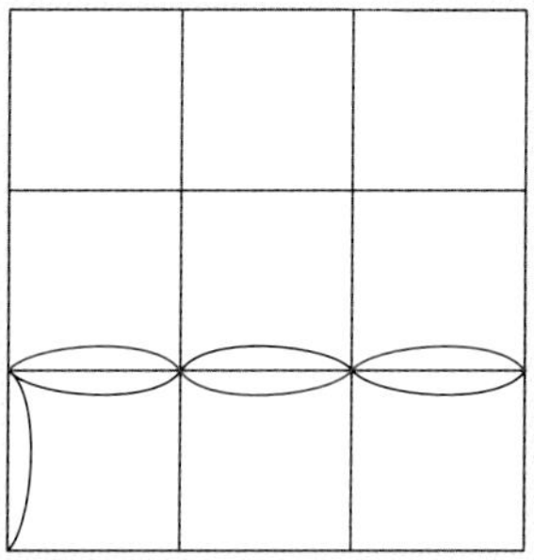

D

STEP 4 Quilt another curved line to the next point above and quilt a serpentine line across and back, as in Steps 2 and 3. *Fig. E*

STEP 5 Quilt another curved line to the upper right corner of the block and over to the next point. *Fig. F*

STEP 6 Quilt a serpentine line to the bottom of the block and back. *Fig. G*

STEP 7 Quilt another line to the next corner and quilt another serpentine line to the bottom and back. *Fig. H*

STEP 8 Quilt a curve to the right upper corner, then along the right side from corner to corner. *Fig. I*

STEP 9 Quilt curves from point to point along the bottom, returning to the original starting point. *Fig. J*

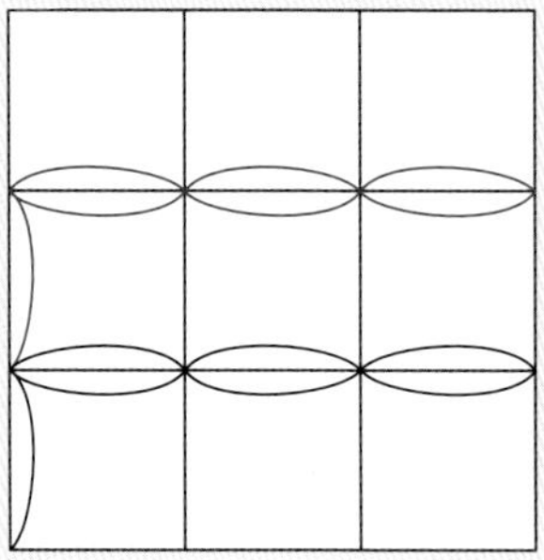
E

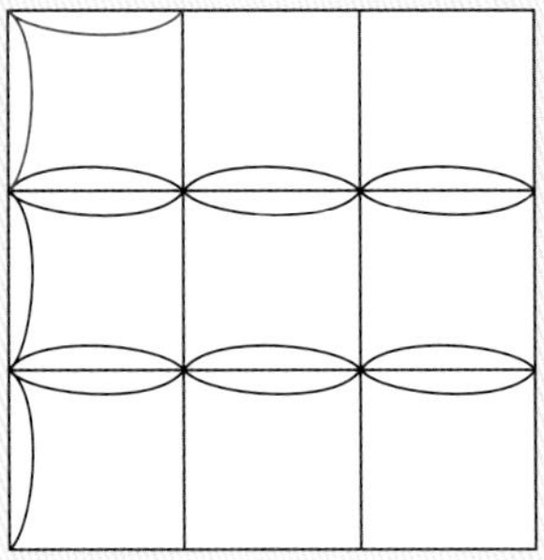
F

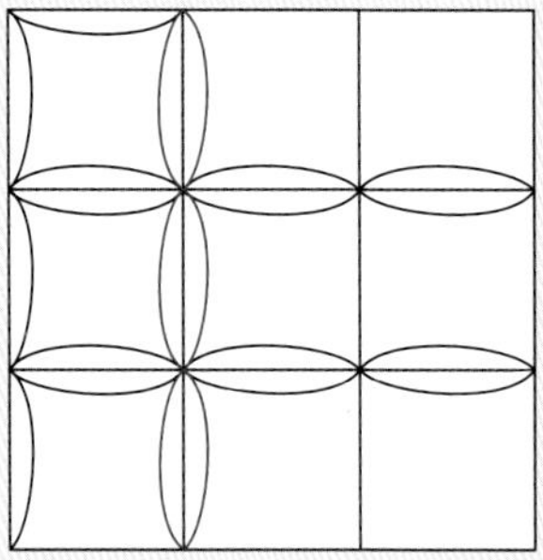
G

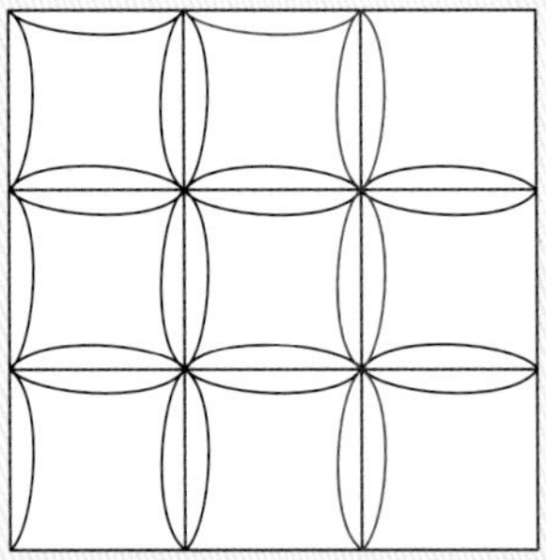
H

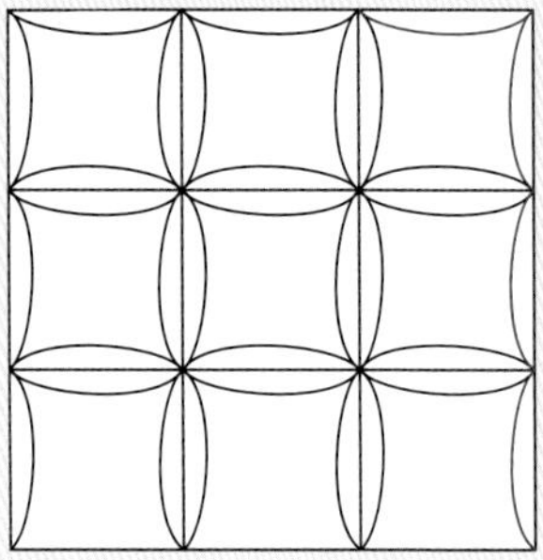
I

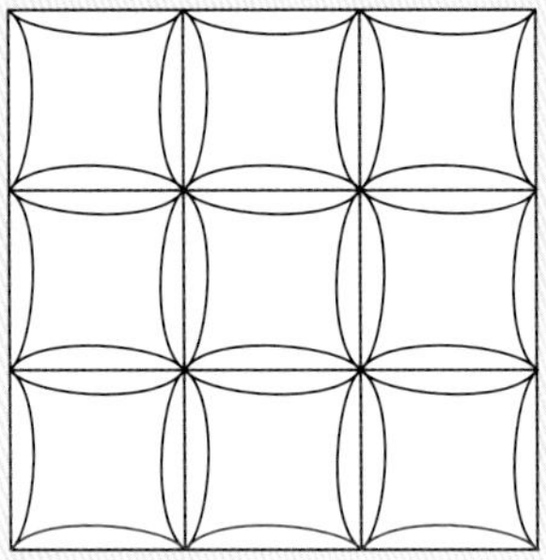
J

BINDING

After quilting, square up and trim the excess batting and backing even with the edge of the quilt top. In this book, almost all the binding strips are cut at 2½″ × width of fabric. Smaller quilts will use a 2¼″ binding. Join the strips with a diagonal seam.

Always press the binding seams open to reduce bulk. Fold the binding in half lengthwise, press, and use your favorite method to sew it to the quilt.

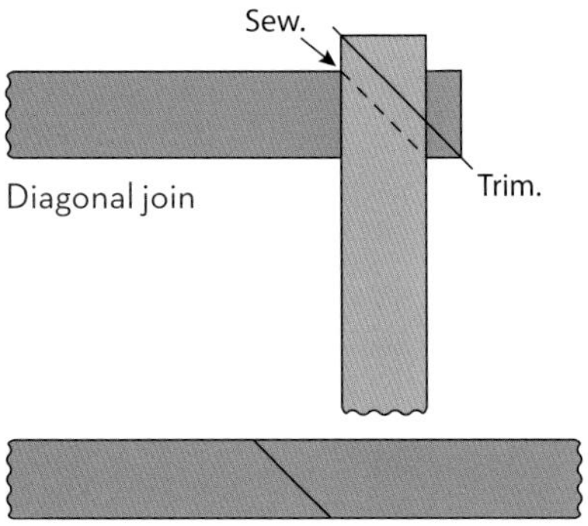

Finished seam

Sky Scrape

FINISHED QUILT: 31½″ × 39″ ■ FINISHED BLOCK: 4½″ × 4½″

The colored fabrics really pop off the dark gray background of this modern Nine-Patch quilt. It's a great way to use scraps or 5″ × 5″ and 10″ × 10″ precut squares.

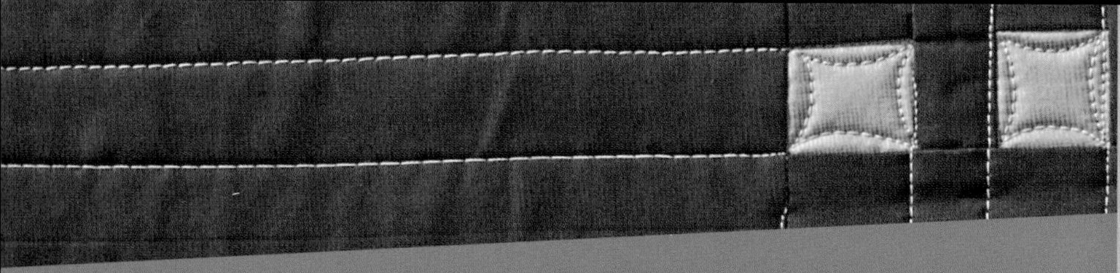

Design Notes

Pick your favorite colors! Any combination of colors in light, medium, and dark works for this quilt.

Fabrics

Yardage is based on 42″ usable fabric width. WOF = width of fabric.

Assorted colors: 9 colors—
1 strip 1½″ × 15″ or
1 square 5″ × 5″ of each color:

- Light pink
- Medium pink
- Hot pink
- Yellow
- Gold
- Orange
- Light blue
- Medium blue
- Dark blue

Assorted neutrals: 3 colors—
1 strip 1½″ × WOF or
1 square 10″ × 10″ of each color:

- Light gray
- Medium gray
- Black

Dark gray: 3⅛ yards for sashing, borders, backing, and binding

Batting: 38″ × 45″

Cutting

ASSORTED COLORS

Cut 9 squares 1½" × 1½" from each color for Nine-Patch blocks.

ASSORTED NEUTRALS

Cut 27 squares 1½" × 1½" from each neutral for Nine-Patch blocks.

DARK GRAY

Cut 9 strips 1¼" × WOF; use 5 strips to subcut 36 rectangles 1¼" × 5" for horizontal block sashing and 4 strips to subcut 108 rectangles 1¼" × 1½" for vertical block sashing.

Your sewn blocks must measure 5" × 5" to use the following sashing strip lengths (see below). If they are not, measure the blocks and cut the 1½"-wide strips to the length that matches the block size. This will give you the measurement for all horizontal sashing rectangles. Once the blocks and sashing rectangles are pieced into columns, measure the height of the column and cut the 1½"-wide strips to that measurement for the vertical sashing.

Sashing:

Cut 4 strips 1½" × WOF; use 2 strips to subcut 1½" × 32½" for vertical sashing and 2 strips to subcut 15 rectangles 1½" × 5" for horizontal sashing.

Borders:

Cut the borders after you complete the quilt top. If your quilt top measures 16" × 32½", cut the border lengths listed below; if it measures smaller or larger than 16" × 32½", refer to Finishing the Quilt, Borders (page 12), to measure and cut the border strips.

Cut 2 strips 8½" × 32½" for side borders.

Cut 1 strip 6½" × 32" for top border.

Cut 1 strip 1½" × 32" for bottom border.

Binding:

Cut 4 strips 2½" × WOF for binding.

Blocks

Use a 1/4″ seam allowance. Refer to Basic Construction (page 8) as needed.

To make each of the 9 Nine-Patch blocks, use 9 of the same-color squares 1 1/2″ × 1 1/2″, 6 vertical block sashing rectangles 1 1/4″ × 1 1/2″, and 2 horizontal block sashing rectangles 1 1/4″ × 5″.

STEP 1 For each block, lay out the squares and sashing rectangles as shown. Starting at the top row, sew 3 colored squares together with 2 dark gray vertical block sashing rectangles 1 1/4″ × 1 1/2″ between them.

5″ × 5″

Press toward the sashing. Repeat to make 3 rows. Sew the dark gray horizontal block sashing rectangles 1 1/4″ × 5″ between the rows. Press. Make 9 blocks with the colored fabrics.

> NOTE
>
> It is easy to accidentally turn the sashing around because the pieces are so close to being square. Be mindful when piecing so that the Nine-Patch block measures 5″ × 5″ at this stage.

STEP 2 Refer to Step 1 to make 3 blocks each of light gray, medium gray, and black (9 blocks).

Assembly

SASHING

STEP 1 Lay out the color blocks in descending order of gradation, 3 colorways across: pink, yellow, and blue. Start with the darkest color on the top, then medium and light, followed by rows of black, medium gray, and light gray on the bottom.

STEP 2 Sew horizontal sashing rectangles 1 1/2″ × 5″ between the blocks to make 3 vertical columns. Press toward the sashing. Join the 3 columns with the 2 vertical sashing strips 1 1/2″ × 32 1/2″ in between. Press toward the sashing.

BORDERS

STEP 1 Sew a side border to each side of the quilt center. Press toward the borders.

STEP 2 Add the top and bottom borders. Press toward the borders.

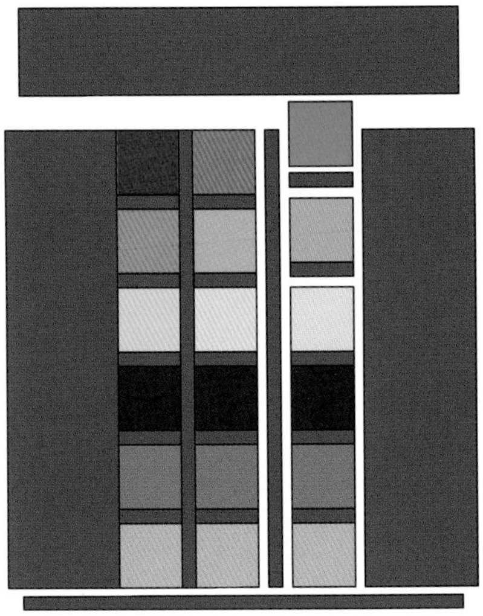

Quilt assembly

Finishing

Refer to Finishing the Quilt (page 12) as needed.

Layer and baste the quilt.

QUILTING

Quilting *Sky Scrape* is the perfect opportunity to use different colors of thread to highlight the Nine-Patch blocks. You can match the threads to all the block colors, or just experiment with a few of your favorites.

Try combining straight lines and continuous curves (page 13) for a fun effect. This also provides great quilting practice, since you quilt a single block at a time. An added bonus is that you use the smaller squares as a guide for the lines, which means no marking.

Straight Lines and Curves

STEP 1 Starting at the edge of the quilt, stitch a straight line that runs along the left side of a Nine-Patch block, stopping at the bottom left corner. Quilt along the bottom of the block and extend the line to the other edge of the quilt. *Fig. A*

STEP 2 Travel 1″ along the edge of the quilt and echo the line quilted in Step 1. Stop at the corner of a block in the Nine-Patch. *Fig. B*

STEP 3 Quilt a line that curves from corner to corner, returning to the first corner. *Fig. C*

STEP 4 Stitch straight across the top of the square until you arrive at the next one, and then quilt another continuous curve. *Fig. D*

STEP 5 Continue quilting continuous curves along the bottom of the block and then along the left side. Stop at the edge of the quilt. *Fig. E*

STEP 6 Repeat Steps 1–5 in the rest of the squares and in other blocks, reversing direction when needed. *Fig. F*

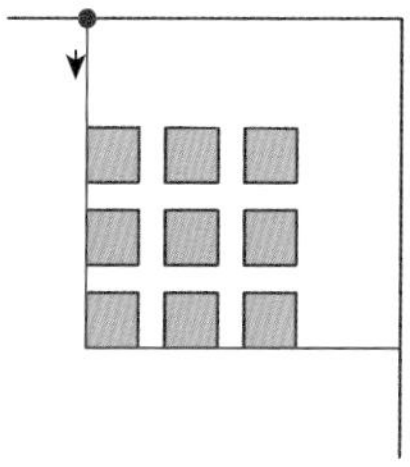

A

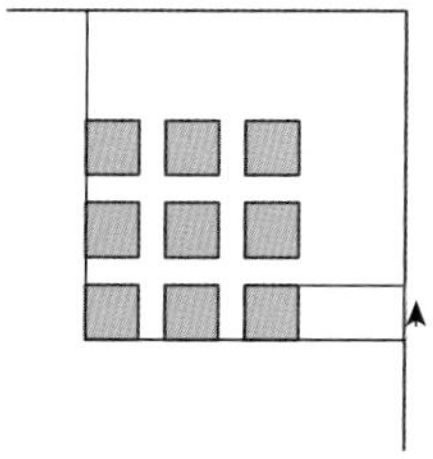

B

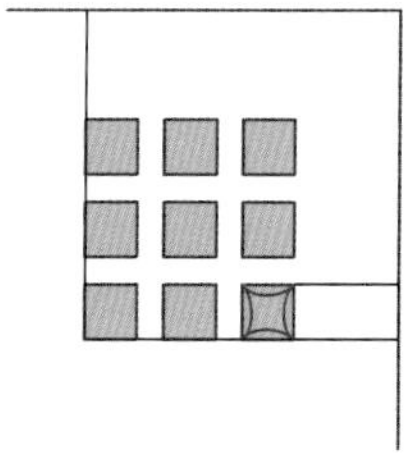

C

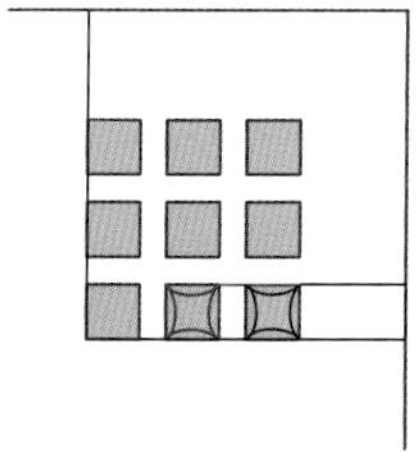

D

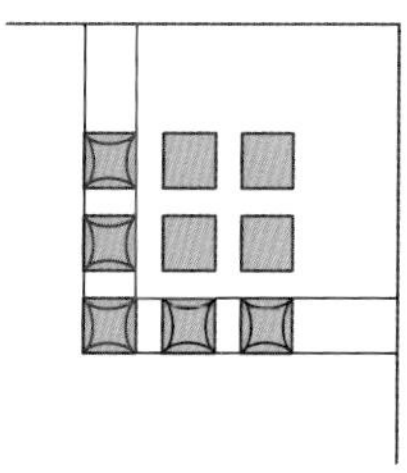

E

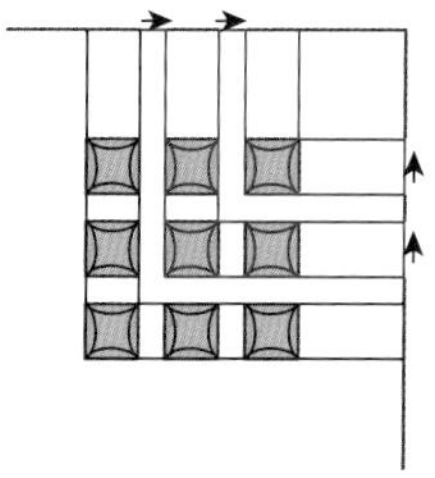

F

THE LAST STEP

Add the binding to your quilt, referring to Binding (page 14) as needed. Note that *Sky Scrape* requires about 155″ of binding.

Union

FINISHED QUILT: 41″ × 59″ ■ FINISHED BLOCK: 6″ × 9″

Guild challenges are a great source of inspiration and an easy excuse to reach outside your comfort zone. An historic building in downtown Kansas City was the inspiration for *Union*. Instead of trying to duplicate features of the building, I was inspired by the colors on the ceiling. Each elongated Nine-Patch block is made using that palette.

Design Notes

Gather a good collection of earth tones and two or three accent colors. Look for solids, near solids, and hand-dyed fabrics. If you use prints, choose ones with small motifs in monotone colors. You don't want bold or high-contrast prints.

Fabrics

Yardage is based on 42″ usable fabric width. WOF = width of fabric.

Earth tones (cream to dark brown): 16–20 fat eighths or 6–10 fat quarters

Accents (orange, blue, and gold): 2–3 fat eighths of each

Cream: 1 yard for sashing and binding

Backing: 2¾ yards

Batting: 47″ × 65″

Cutting

ASSORTED EARTH TONES AND ACCENT FABRICS

Cut a total of 324 rectangles 2½″ × 3½″.

CREAM

Sashing:

Cut 13 strips 1½″ × WOF; subcut 8 strips into 30 vertical sashing strips 1½″ × 9½″. Set aside the remaining 5 strips 1½″ × WOF for horizontal sashing.

Binding:

Cut 5 strips 2½″ × WOF.

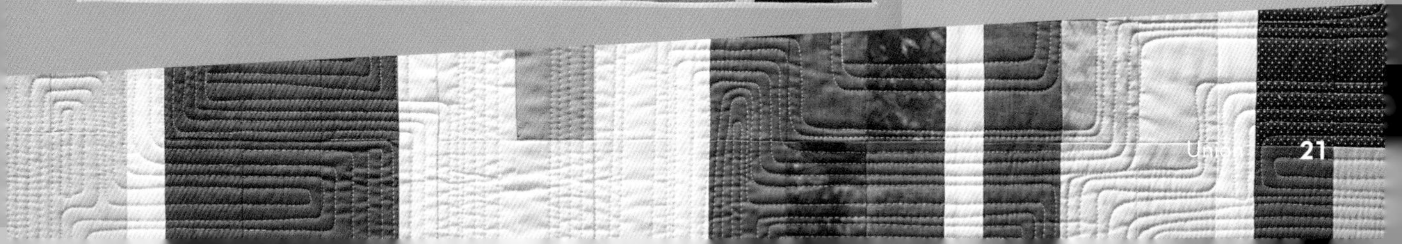

Blocks

Use a 1/4″ seam allowance. Refer to Basic Construction (page 8) as needed.

Each of the 36 blocks is made of 9 small 2½″ × 3½″ rectangles. Sew 3 rectangles together along their 3½″ sides to make a row 6½″ × 3½″. Next sew 3 rows to each other along their 6½″ widths to make a large Nine-Patch rectangle block that measures 6½″ × 9½″.

The blocks are improv-pieced, meaning they are made without a road map. You decide how each block looks as you make it. Don't think ahead too far and don't question your decisions too critically. The fun is in trusting your intuition and fabrics to create a one-of-a-kind piece of art!

Start by cutting many 2½″ × 3½″ units of the main fabrics and fewer of the accent fabrics. Having a lot of precut rectangles frees you to make decisions faster and to be more spur of the moment.

Each block should be a small piece of art, but it will also react to the adjacent blocks. Keep that in mind, but don't dwell on it as you put together the rectangles. You want the colors of blocks to flow across the top, but in an organic way—you don't want them to look too planned.

NOTE

You aren't limited to 9 solid rectangles per block. Try piecing together small scraps and trimming the unit to 2½″ × 3½″ to add more texture and visual interest to the block.

As you determine color placement for each block, sew the blocks. Make 36.

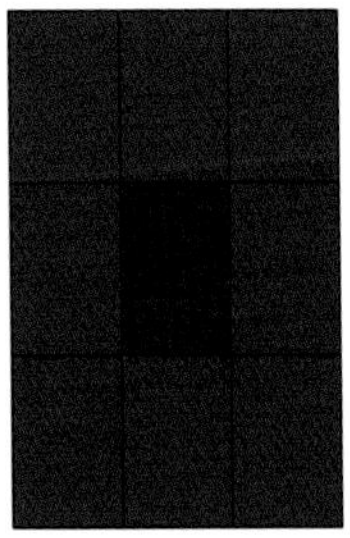

6½″ × 9½″

Assembly

Lay out the blocks in 6 rows of 6 blocks each. Again, don't think too much about the placement—think only about the flow. Make sure the blocks flow from one to the next in a pleasing way.

SASHING

STEP 1 Sew 1½″ × 9½″ vertical sashing strips in between the blocks. Press toward the sashing.

STEP 2 Piece together the horizontal sashing strips and cut into 41½″ strips. Sew the rows together with the horizontal sashing in between.

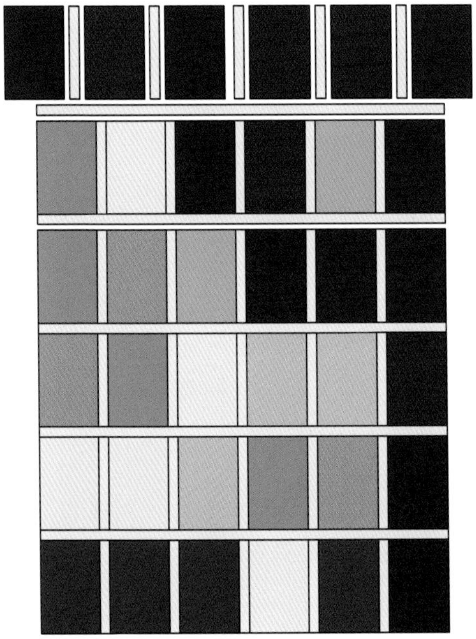

Quilt assembly

Finishing

Refer to Finishing the Quilt (page 12) as needed.

Layer and baste the quilt.

QUILTING

The quilting designs you use can add texture, provide movement, and can even help show the inspiration behind the quilt. *Union*, inspired by an historic train station, provides all sorts of quilting options. Quilting multiple train tracks that lead to one block is a playful way to hint at that inspiration. It doesn't have to be a graphic representation. You're the only person who has to understand the reasoning!

Railroads

Quilt the railroads so that they radiate from a single block, just like a real union station. Or quilt them randomly over the whole area—the choice is yours!

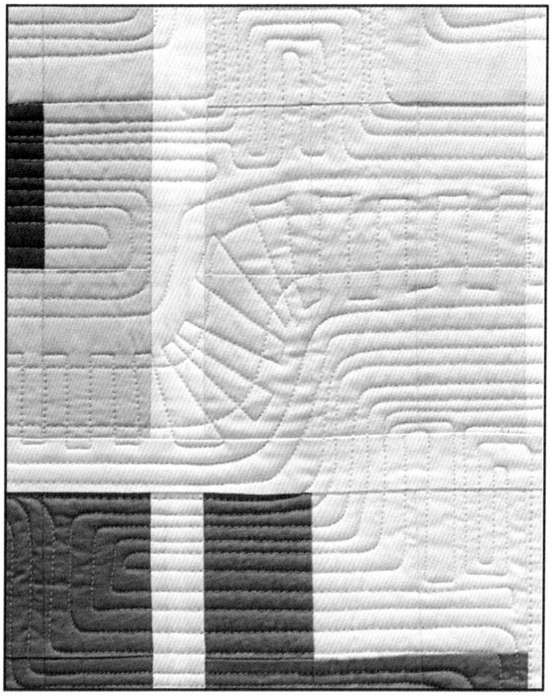

STEP 1 Starting from the edge of a block, quilt a line that gently curves to the edge of the quilt or the edge of another block. *Fig. A*

STEP 2 Travel along the edge 1½″–2″ and echo the line back to the block. *Fig. B*

STEP 3 Quilt along the edge of the block until you are ½″ above the first quilted line. Quilt away from the block about ½″ and then down across the 2 lines, stopping ½″ below. *Fig. C*

STEP 4 Quilt away from the block another ½″ and then up across the 2 lines, stopping ½″ above. *Fig. D*

STEP 5 Continue quilting straight lines that travel across the 2 lines, alternating sides. When quilting around curves, some lines may be closer together or further apart. Remember, you are just hinting at the inspiration behind the quilt, not making a realistic representation. *Fig. E*

In the rest of the area, you can quilt echoed lines or another type of quilting design. Just be sure not to leave any huge gaps in the quilting!

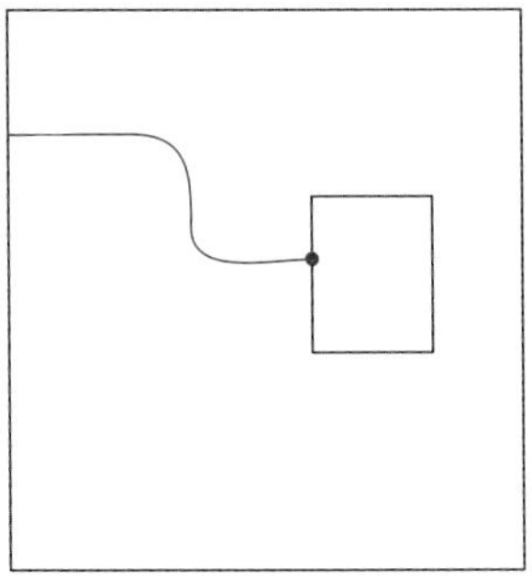

A

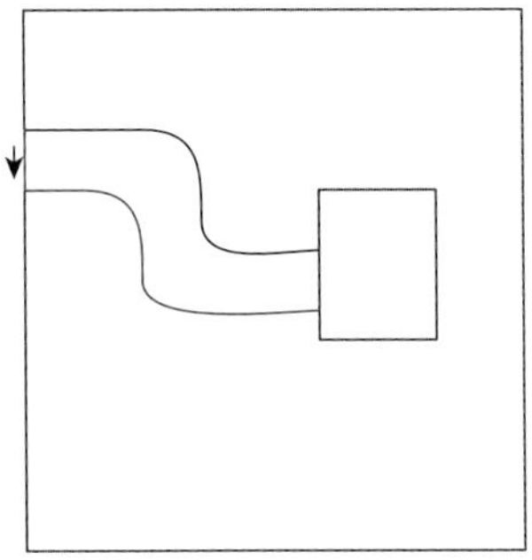

B

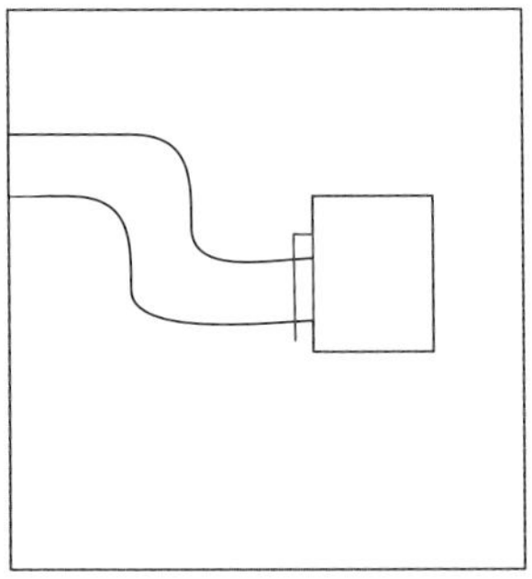

C

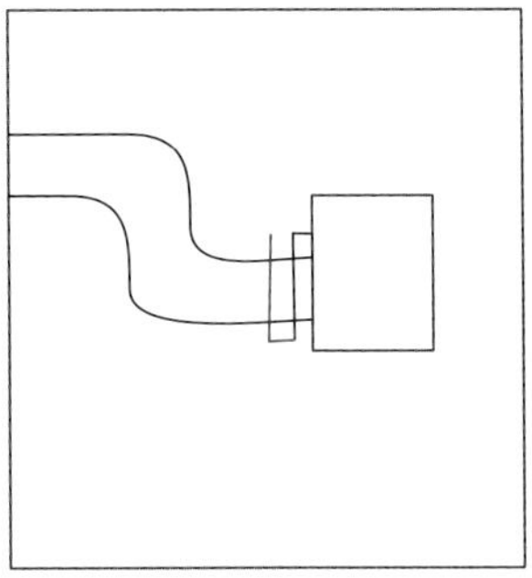

D

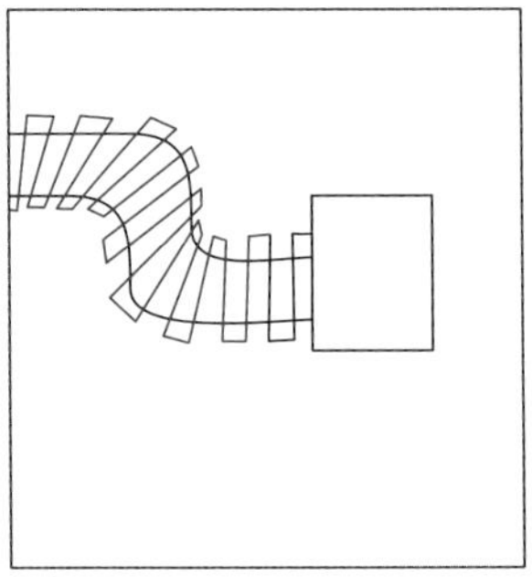

E

THE LAST STEP

Add the binding to your quilt, referring to Binding (page 14) as needed. Note that *Union* requires about 215″ of binding.

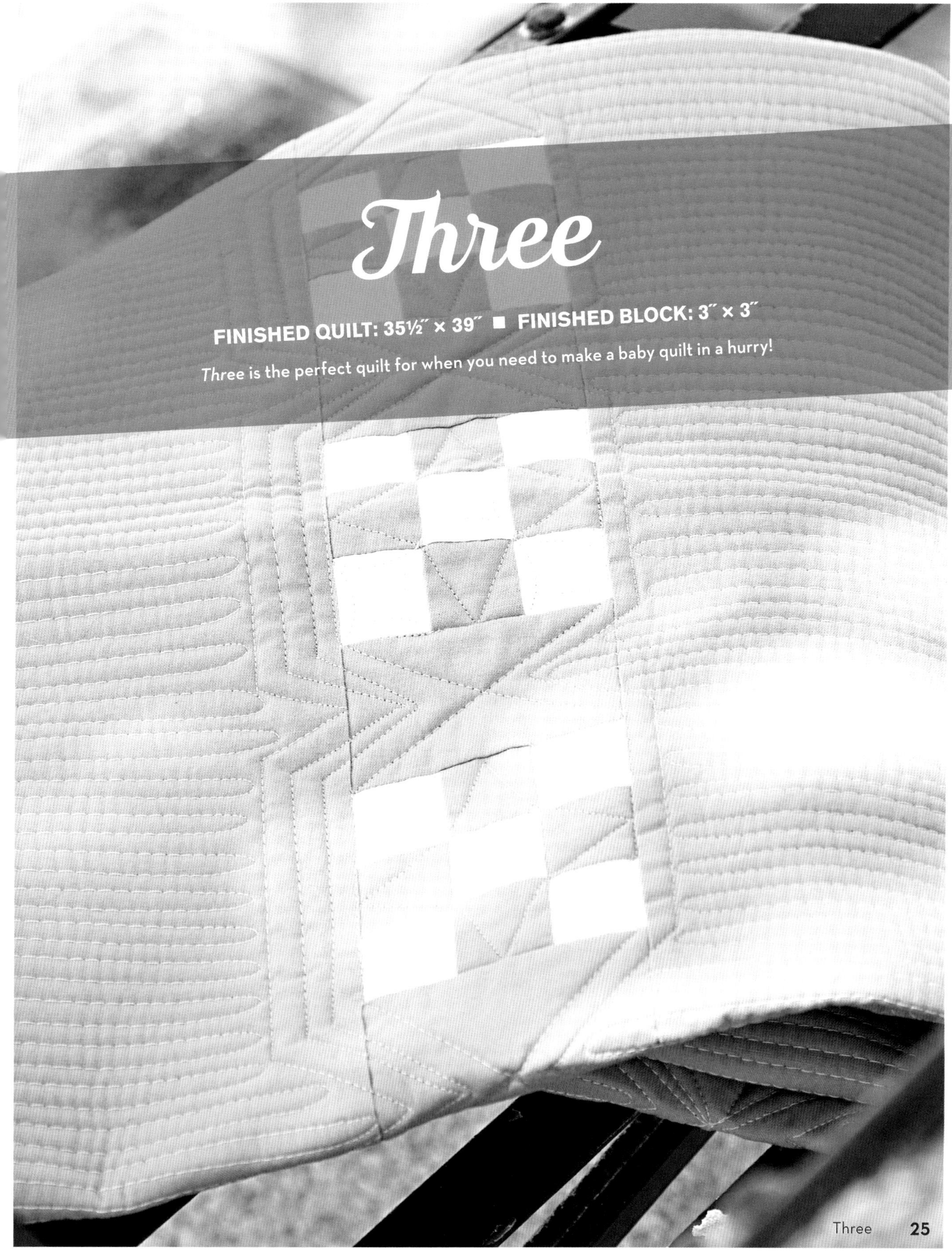

Three

FINISHED QUILT: 35½″ × 39″ ■ FINISHED BLOCK: 3″ × 3″

Three is the perfect quilt for when you need to make a baby quilt in a hurry!

Design Notes

The flange in the binding adds a little bit of color and style to the quilt, but you can leave out that detail to make the quilt come together even faster!

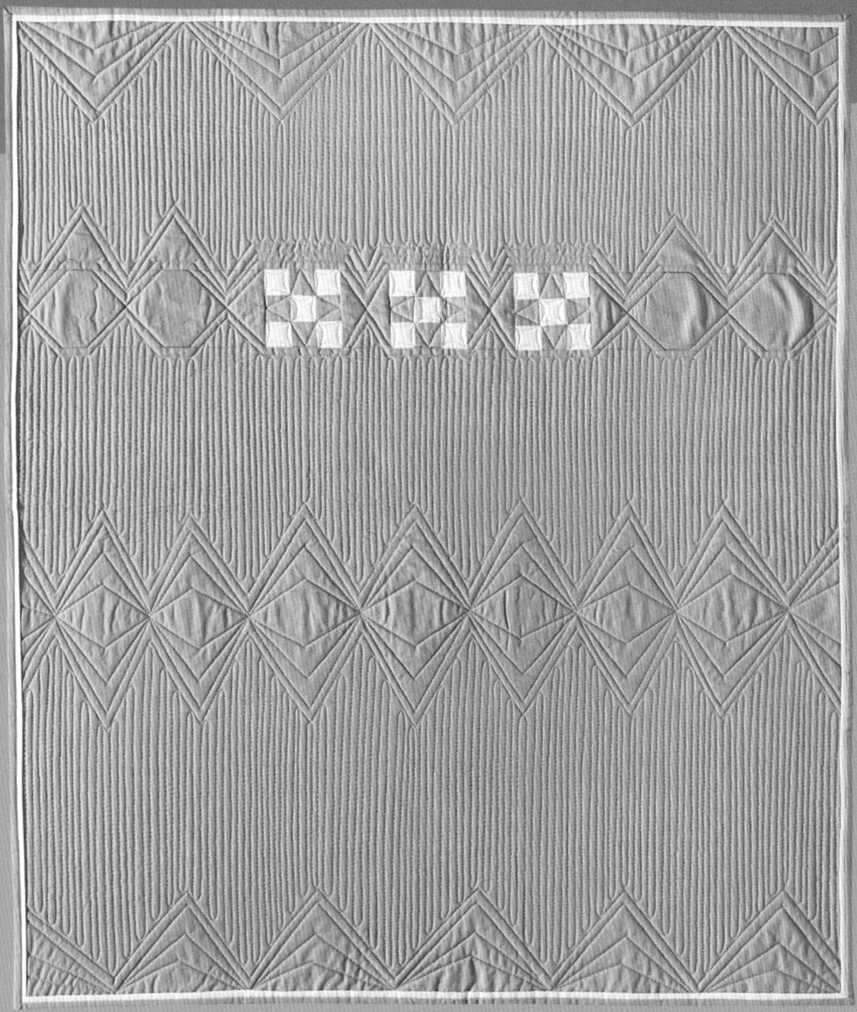

Fabrics

Yardage is based on 42″ usable fabric width. WOF = width of fabric; LOF = length of fabric.

Note: The width of the binding and the batting and backing requirements have been reduced because of the small size of the quilt.

Blue: 2⅝ yards for top, backing, and binding

White: ¼ yard

Batting: 42″ × 45″

Cutting

BLUE

Cut 1⅜ yards for backing.

Cut 4 strips 2″ × WOF for binding.

Cut 1 strip 36″ × WOF.

- Subcut LOF 1 strip 1½″ × 36″; subcut 12 squares 1½″ × 1½″ for blocks.
- Subcut LOF 1 strip 3½″ × 36″; subcut 2 strips 3½″ × 15½″ and 2 rectangles 2½″ × 3½″.
- Subcut 1 strip 10½″ × 36″ for top border.
- Reserve remaining 26½″ × 36″ piece for quilt bottom.

WHITE

Cut 1 strip 1½″ × WOF; subcut 15 squares 1½″ × 1½″ for blocks.

Cut 4 strips 1″ × WOF for flange.

Blocks

Use a ¼″ seam allowance. Refer to Basic Construction (page 8) as needed.

Using 5 white squares and 4 blue squares in each block, make 3 Nine-Patch blocks.

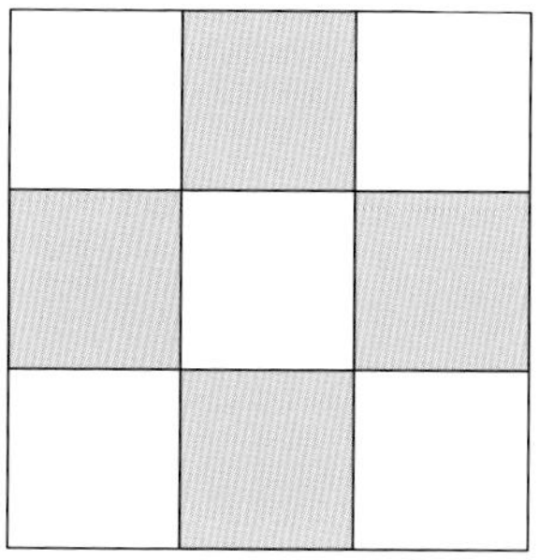

3½″ × 3½″

Assembly

STEP 1 Sew 2 rectangles 2½″ × 3½″ between the 3 Nine-Patch blocks. Press toward the rectangles.

STEP 2 Sew 2 strips 3½″ × 15½″ to each side of the pieced block unit.

STEP 3 Center and sew the 10½″ border strip to the top of the pieced unit. Trim edges to 36″. Sew the reserved piece to the bottom.

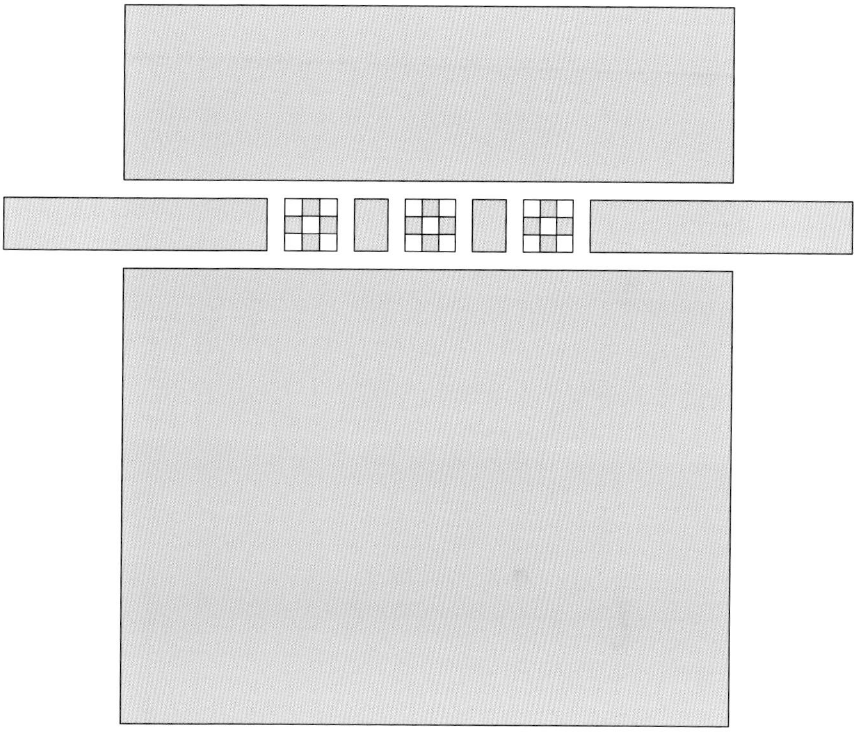

Quilt assembly

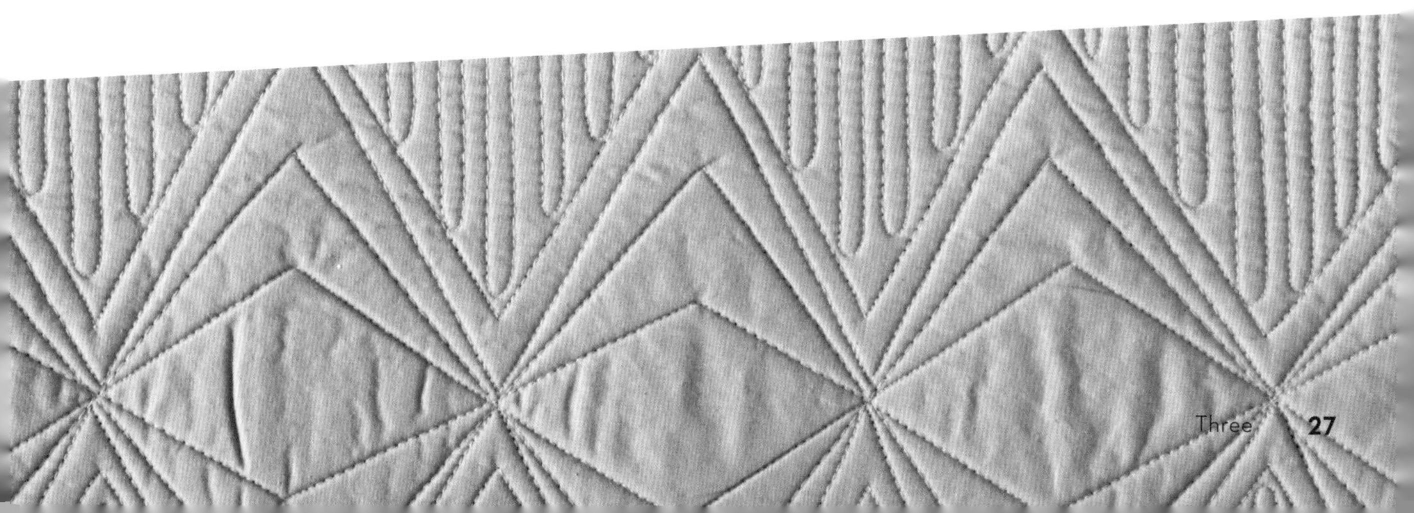

Finishing

Refer to Finishing the Quilt (page 12) as needed.

Layer and baste the quilt.

QUILTING

The more basic the quilt, the more opportunity there is for quilting fun. In this quilt, you can create secondary designs and break up larger areas just by using echoing. This can make working your way around an area more manageable and less overwhelming.

In the Blocks

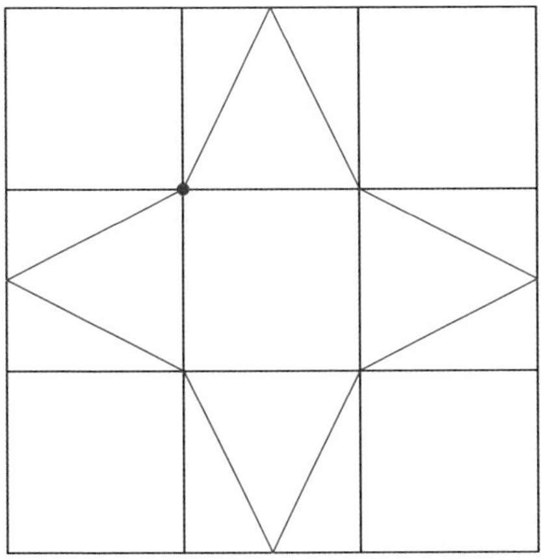

A

B

Incorporating straight and curved lines in the Nine-Patches can result in a complex-looking design that is actually easy to quilt.

STEP 1 Starting at a corner of the middle square of the Nine-Patch block, quilt a diagonal line that extends to the midpoint on the side of the block, and then to the next corner of the center square. Repeat, working around the block and returning to the starting point. *Fig. A*

STEP 2 Quilt continuous curves (page 13) in the rest of the squares. *Fig. B*

Between the Blocks

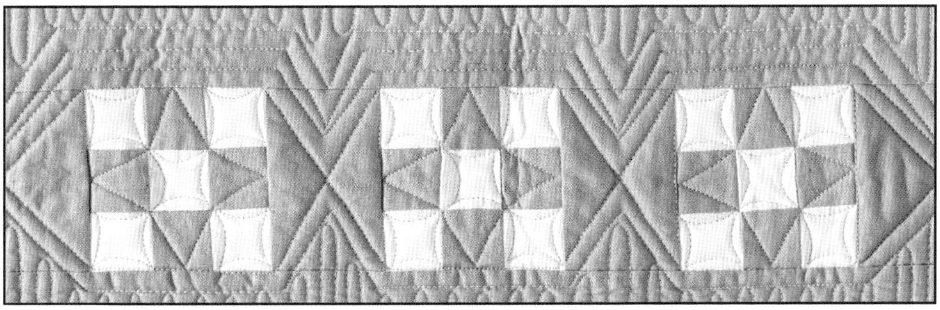

STEP 1 Join together the blocks by quilting an X in between each block. This helps connect the blocks. You can continue it beyond the block area if you like how it looks.

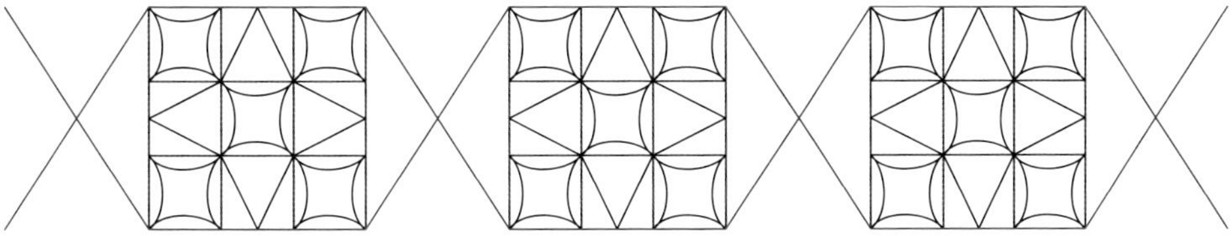

STEP 2 Echo the whole section to separate it from the rest of the quilting.

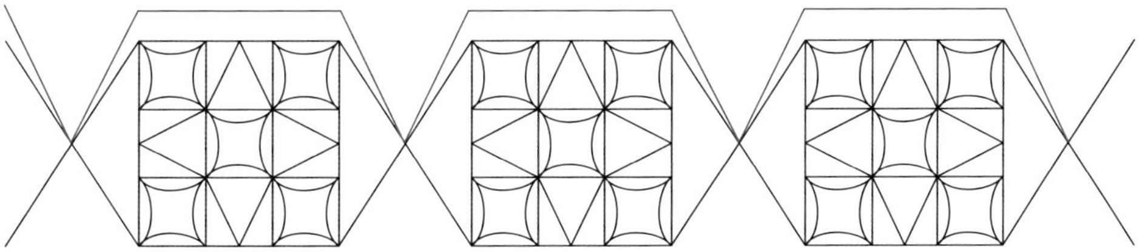

Echo it as many times as you like. Try 1, 2, or even 3 echo lines for different looks.

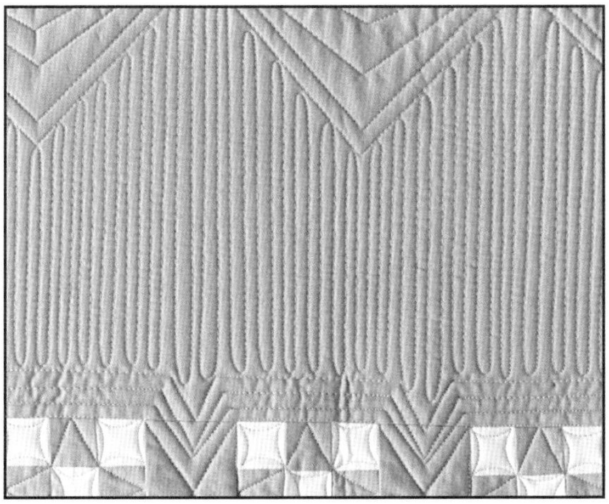

Blocks with 1 echo line under

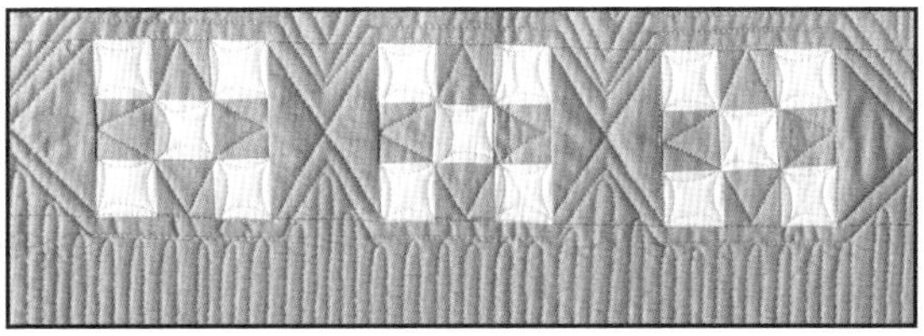

Blocks with 3 echo lines

> NOTE
>
> A machine-quilting ruler helps keep the lines straight-ish and can be used on a stand-up quilting machine or a domestic sewing machine (with the proper foot).

Negative Space

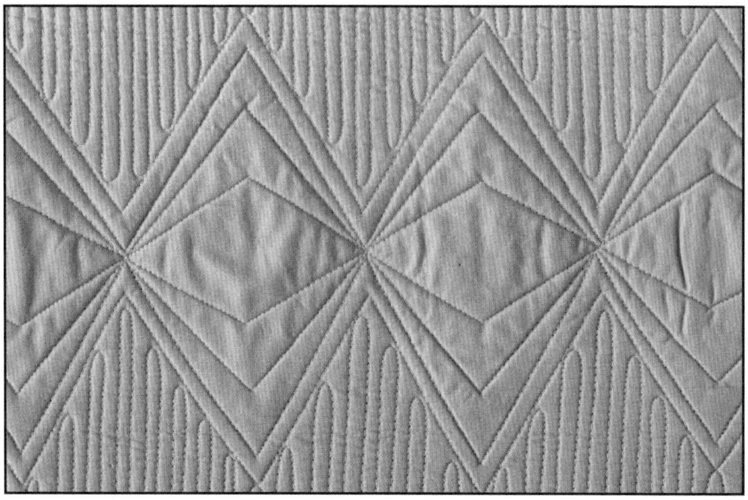

Using the quilting to create "blocks" on the quilt is a great way to break up large areas.

STEP 1 Mark out the first basic shape, a row of squares on point. *Fig. A*

STEP 2 Use the lines as reference points to fill in the rest of the design, referring to the diagrams. *Figs. B & C*

Remember that echoing is a great way to show off your designs. Echo the shapes to keep them from blending in with the rest of the quilting. *Fig. D*

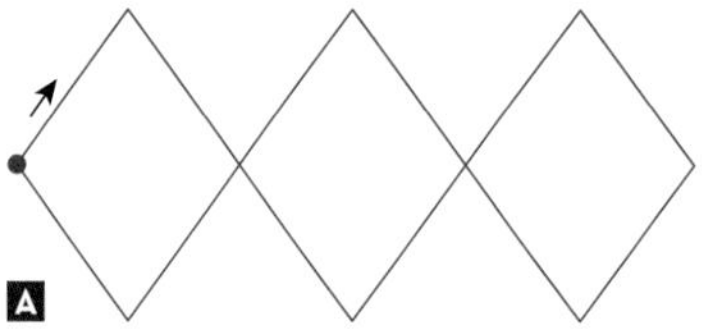

A

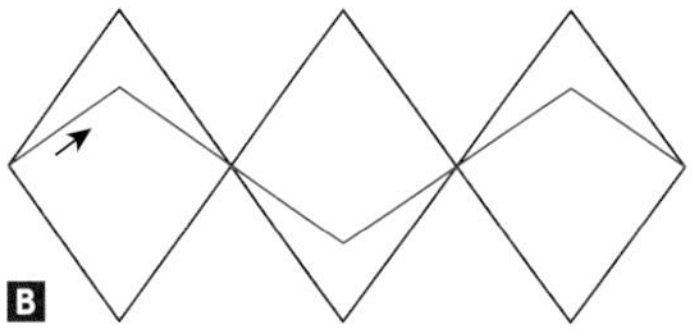

B

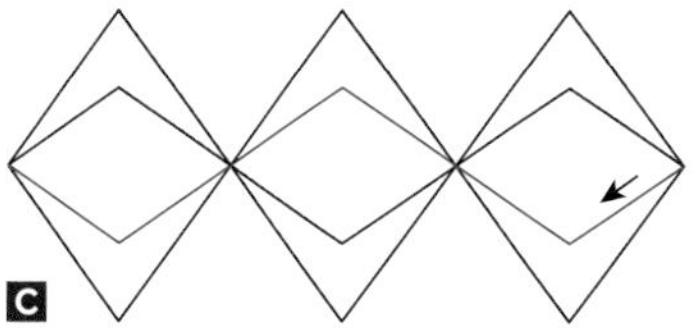

C

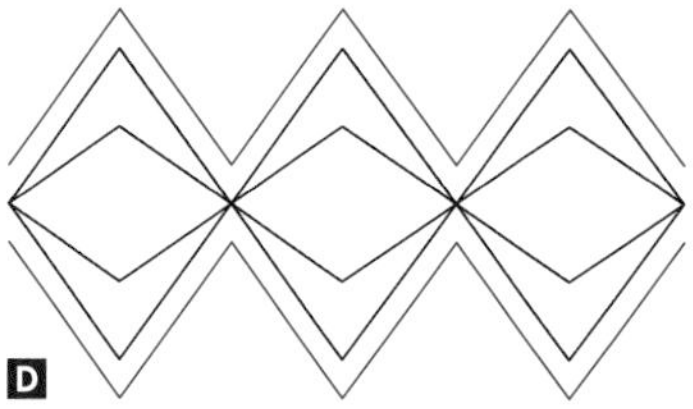

D

THE LAST STEP

STEP 1 To make the flange, measure the quilt through the center from top to bottom and side to side. Cut 2 white 1″ accent strips of each measurement.

STEP 2 Press the strips in half lengthwise. Pin the flange to the outside edges of the quilt, all raw edges matching. Overlap the strips at the corners.

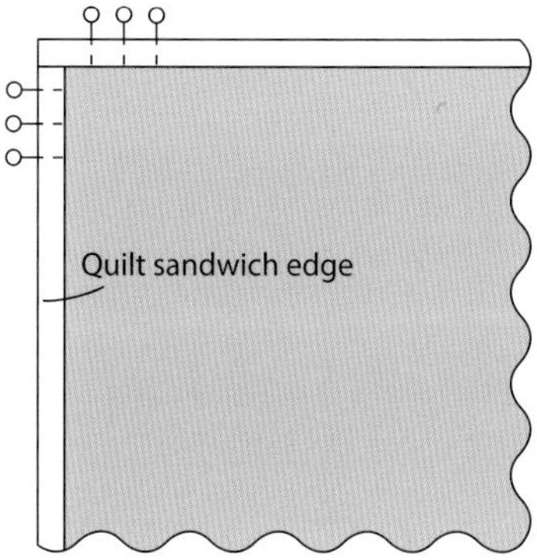

STEP 3 Bind the quilt as usual, making sure the accent color peeks out from underneath the binding.

STEP 4 Add the binding to your quilt, referring to Binding (page 14) as needed. Note that *Three* requires about 175″ of blue binding.

Nine-Patch X

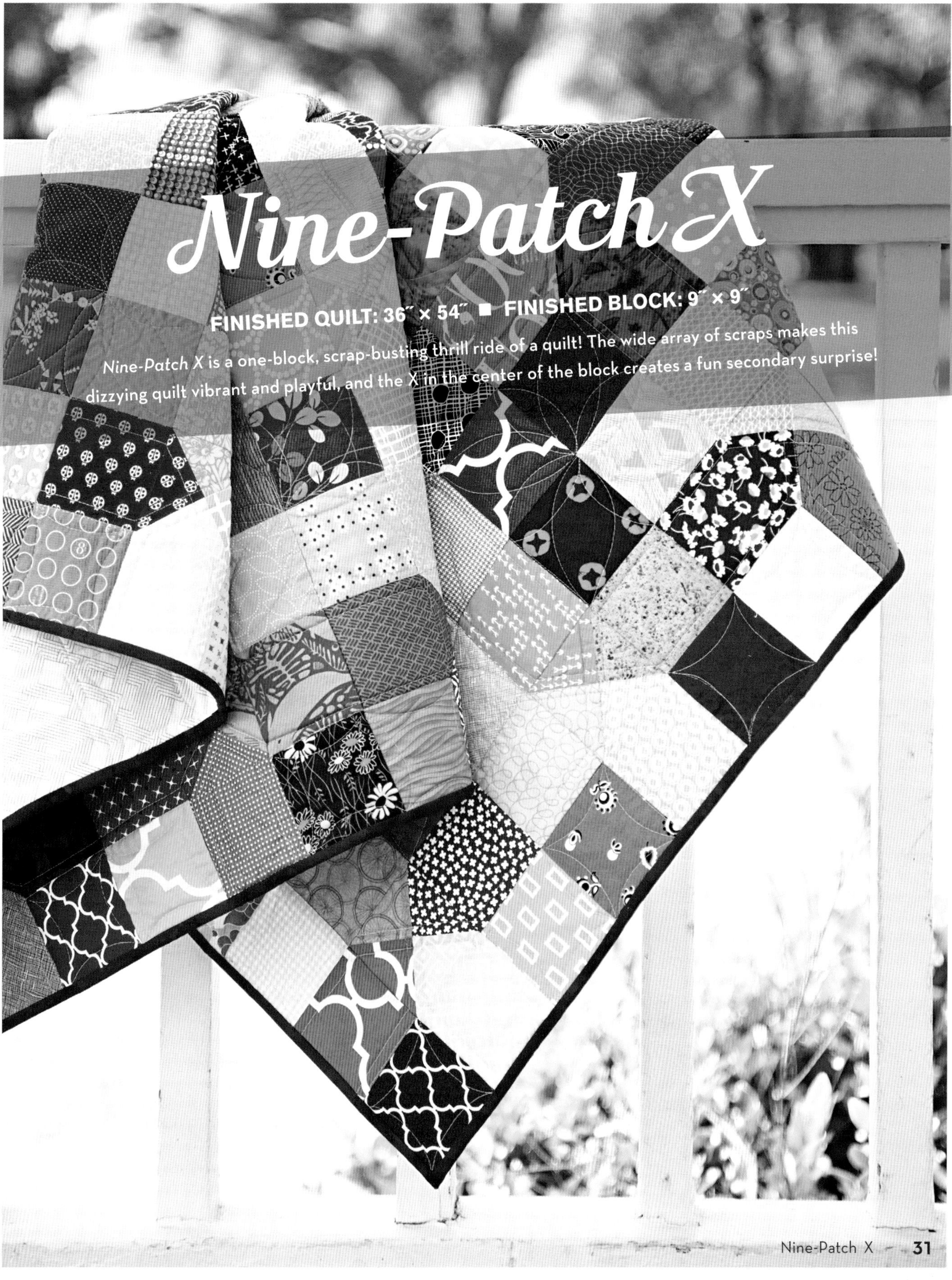

FINISHED QUILT: 36″ × 54″ ■ FINISHED BLOCK: 9″ × 9″

Nine-Patch X is a one-block, scrap-busting thrill ride of a quilt! The wide array of scraps makes this dizzying quilt vibrant and playful, and the X in the center of the block creates a fun secondary surprise!

Design Notes

Up to 192 different scraps can be used in this quilt, making it a great project for a fabric swap with friends. You can swap 10″ × 10″ squares or 3½″ × 3½″ squares for maximum scrappiness!

Fabrics

Yardage is based on 42″ usable fabric width. WOF = width of fabric.

Prints: Up to 192 different scraps in all colors of the rainbow (plus black and gray), including:

- 96 random scraps at least 3½″ × 3½″
- 96 matching scraps at least 6″ × 10″

Black (or other solid): ½ yard for binding

Print: 1¾ yard for backing

Batting: 42″ × 60″

Cutting

ASSORTED PRINT SCRAPS

Random scraps:

Cut 96 squares 3½″ × 3½″.

Matching scraps:

Cut 96 squares 3½″ × 3½″.

Cut 96 squares 4¼″ × 4¼″.

Cut each 4¼″ × 4¼″ square on the diagonal twice to make 4 triangles. There will be 3 remaining triangles you can use for another project.

> **NOTE**
>
> If you want room to trim the quarter-square triangle units, cut the matching squares 4½″ × 4½″.

BINDING

Cut 5 strips 2½″ × WOF.

Blocks

Use a 1/4″ seam allowance. Refer to Basic Construction (page 8) as needed.

Each block is made of 8 squares and 1 quarter-square triangle unit.

STEP 1 Lay out 4 different quarter-square triangles. Sew the triangles together in pairs as shown and join the pairs. Trim to 3½″ × 3½″ if necessary. Make 24.

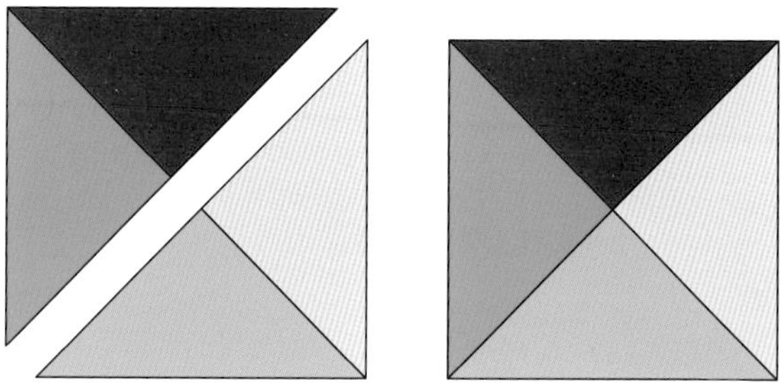

3½″ × 3½″

STEP 2 Lay out the quarter-square triangle unit and place the matching 3½″ × 3½″ scrap squares next to the corresponding triangles. Fill in the corners with random 3½″ × 3½″ scrap squares. Sew them together in rows, and then join the rows. Make 24.

9½″ × 9½″

Assembly

STEP 1 Lay out the blocks in 6 rows of 4 blocks each. Try to keep matching colors from touching each other if possible. (It's okay if some touch.)

STEP 2 Sew the blocks together in rows, and then join the rows.

Quilt assembly

> **NOTE**
>
> This quilt is easily scalable since the finished blocks are 9″ × 9″. Increase or decrease by multiples of 9 to create the size you want.

Finishing

Refer to Finishing the Quilt (page 12) as needed.

Layer and baste the quilt.

QUILTING

The planned scrappiness of *Nine-Patch X* provides the perfect pieced reference points for fun, fast quilting. Use a variation of the continuous curve (page 13) for a design that looks more complex than it is!

Flower Design

> NOTE
>
> You can start this design from the center, but if you start from an edge, you'll end up on the edge of the block, allowing you to move on to the next block without breaking the thread.

STEP 1 Starting from the middle of the left side of the block, quilt a line that curves to the center where the squares meet. *Fig. A*

STEP 2 Quilt a line that curves out to the upper left corner of the block, and then return to the center point. *Fig. B*

STEP 3 Quilt another line that curves out to the top middle of the block, returning to the center. *Fig. C*

STEP 4 Repeat this process to quilt the upper right portion of the block and then the bottom half of the block, returning to the same point you started. *Figs. D & E*

THE LAST STEP

Add the binding to your quilt, referring to Binding (page 14) as needed. Note that *Nine-Patch X* requires about 200″ of binding.

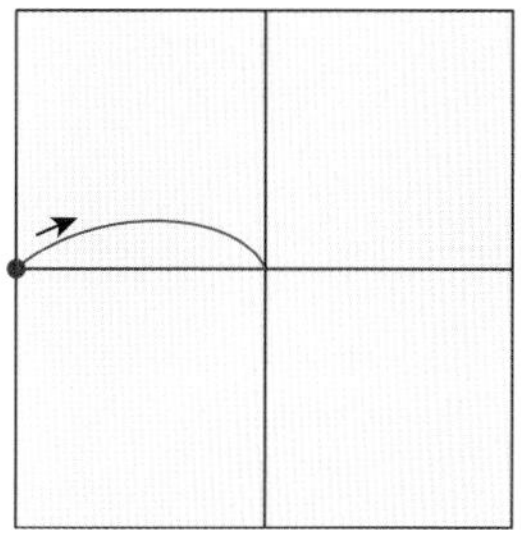

A

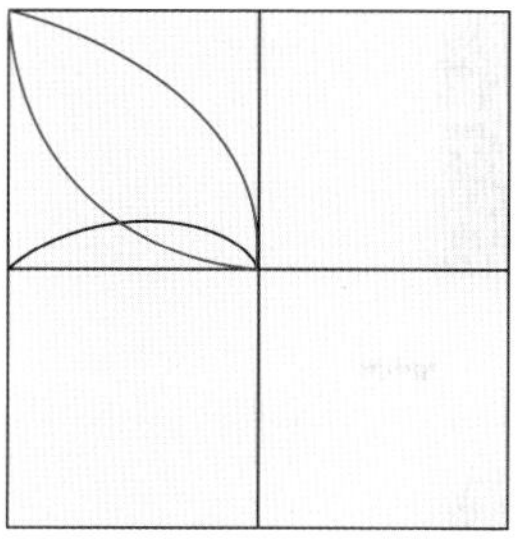

B

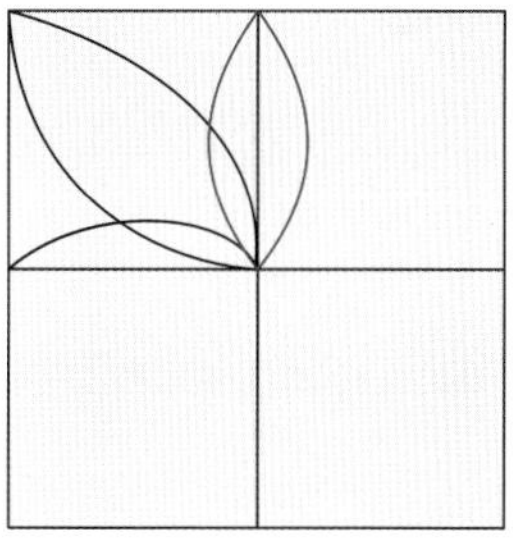

C

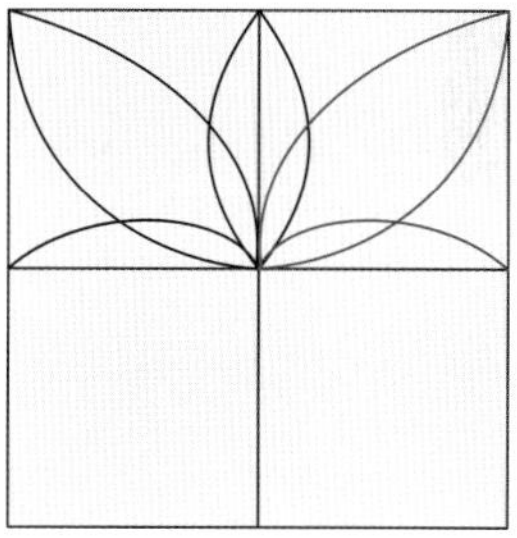

D

E

Color Blocks

FINISHED QUILT: 36″ × 45″ ■ FINISHED BLOCK: 9″ × 9″

Color Blocks is a super-simple, bright, and playful design for when you need a special baby quilt! It comes together in an afternoon, and the large expanses of color give you ample room to practice quilting.

Design Notes

The light gray fabric used for the modified Nine-Patch blocks can all be the same, or you can use up to 6 different light grays. Check your stash to see if you can use what you already have.

Fabrics

Yardage is based on 42″ usable fabric width. WOF = width of fabric.

Yellow, purple, hot pink, and green: ⅓ yard of each

Blue and orange: 1 fat quarter of each

Light gray: *Either 1 gray* (½ yard or 2 different fat quarters) *or 6 different grays* (11″ × 11″ squares of each fabric)

Dark gray: 2 yards for backing and binding

Batting: 42″ × 51″

Cutting

COLOR FABRICS

From each color:

Cut 1 square 9½″ × 9½″.

Cut 1 square 3½″ × 3½″.

YELLOW, PURPLE, HOT PINK, AND GREEN

From each of these colors:

Cut 1 rectangle 9½″ × 18½″.

LIGHT GRAY

If using only 1 gray:

Cut 4 strips 3½″ × WOF; subcut 12 rectangles 3½″ × 9½″ and 12 squares 3½″ × 3½″.

If using 6 different grays:

You'll need a total of 12 rectangles and 12 squares. From each gray:

Cut 2 rectangles 3½″ × 9½″.

Cut 2 squares 3½″ × 3½″.

BINDING

Cut 5 strips 2½″ × WOF.

Blocks

Use a ¼″ seam allowance. Refer to Basic Construction (page 8) as needed.

From each color, make a modified Nine-Patch using the colored 3½″ × 3½″ square, 2 long gray rectangles, and 2 gray squares.

STEP 1 Sew 2 gray squares to either side of the colored square.

STEP 2 Sew 2 gray rectangles to either side of this unit. *Fig. A*

Make 1 block of each color.

STEP 3 Join the corresponding modified Nine-Patch block to its 9½″ × 9½″ square. *Fig. B*

Make 1 block in each color. Set aside the blue and orange blocks.

STEP 4 Join the corresponding 9½″ × 18½″ rectangles to their Step 3 units. Make 1 block each for yellow, purple, hot pink, and green. *Fig. C*

Quilt Top Assembly

STEP 1 Lay out all blocks in your desired configuration.

STEP 2 Sew them together in 3 rows of 2 blocks. *Fig. D*

Finishing

Refer to Finishing the Quilt (page 12) as needed.

Layer and baste the quilt.

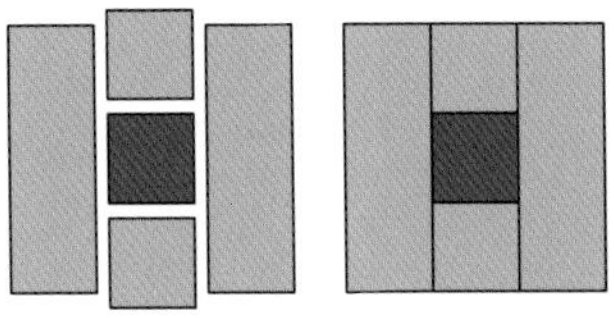

A 9½″ × 9½″

B 18½″ × 9½″

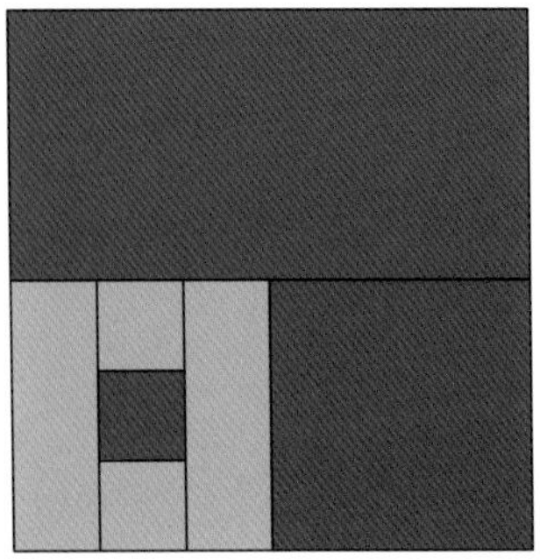

C 18½″ × 18½″

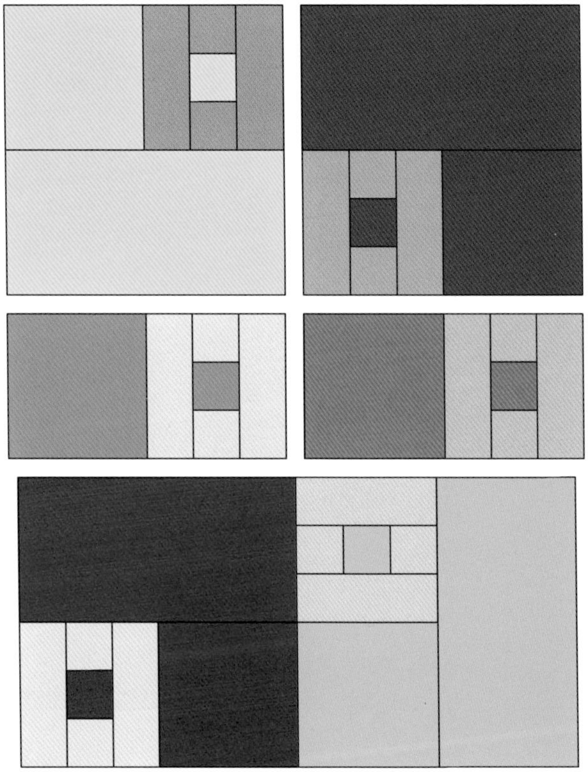

D Quilt assembly

QUILTING

Big blocks are the perfect canvas to practice several different types of quilting designs. In fact, you can view this quilt as a "quilting sampler." You can practice designs you want to perfect or use this quilt as a chance to show off your awesome quilting skills.

Just a few of the quilting options available include a basic meander, leafy meander, wavy lines, loopy meander, or even some boxy squares.

Tip

Using a thinner thread (such as a 50-weight) and matching the thread to the fabric keeps all the different designs from overwhelming the quilt top.

Meander Leafy meander Wavy lines

Pieced Block

Even though the gray blocks are pieced to look like a solid block, you can still quilt the pieces as though they were individual blocks. It's easy and shows off the Nine-Patch theme behind the quilt.

You can have fun with the block by quilting a different design in the center. Combining curvy lines with a more geometrical shape in the center is a perfect way to highlight the pop of color.

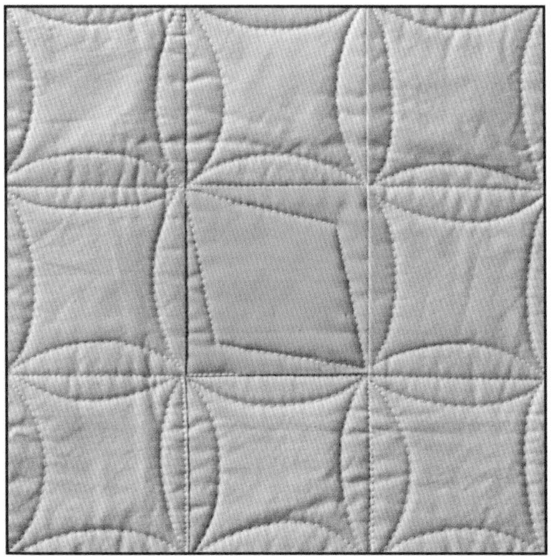

STEP 1 Starting from a corner of the center square, quilt a diamond that extends to the opposite corner, then returns to the starting point. *Fig. A*

STEP 2 Quilt a series of continuous curves (page 13), filling in the rest of the block. *Fig. B*

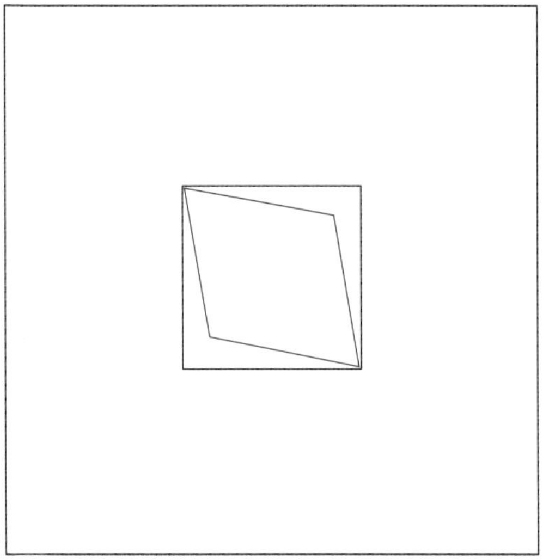

A

B

THE LAST STEP

Add the binding to your quilt, referring to Binding (page 14) as needed. Note that *Color Blocks* requires about 180″ of binding.

Starburst

FINISHED QUILT: 36″ × 51″ ■ FINISHED BLOCK: 15″ × 15″

This baby quilt is a fun, unique quilt that will stretch the confident beginner and delight the more experienced quilter. Each block has four identical paper-pieced sections that are sewn with a 3″ Nine-Patch in the center. The block is then put together with partial seams. The Nine-Patch in the center of each block anchors the dizzying, mesmerizing optical illusion once all six blocks are joined together.

Design Notes

Look for two high-contrast, solid colors to use in your quilt. You want the points at the corners of the Nine-Patches to be crisp and sharp. If you choose a small tonal print, make a practice block first and view it from a distance to make sure the points are visible.

Fabrics and Tools

Yardage is based on 42″ usable fabric width. WOF = width of fabric.

Orange: $3\frac{3}{8}$ yards for blocks, borders, and binding

Light gray: 3 yards for blocks, pieced border

Backing: $1\frac{3}{4}$ yards

Batting: 42″ × 57″

Carol Doak's Foundation Paper (from C&T Publishing)

Cutting

BLOCKS AND BORDERS

Orange:

Cut 7 strips $1\frac{1}{2}$″ × WOF; use 2 strips to subcut $1\frac{1}{2}$″ × $1\frac{1}{2}$″ squares to yield 30 squares for the Nine-Patches. The remaining strips will be used later to make the pieced borders.

> **NOTE**
>
> You need only 2–3 squares from the second orange strip. The rest of the strip will be used to make the pieced border.

Light gray:

Cut 7 strips $1\frac{1}{2}$″ × WOF; use 1 strip to subcut $1\frac{1}{2}$″ × $1\frac{1}{2}$″ squares to yield 24 squares for the Nine-Patches. The remaining strips will be used later to make the pieced borders.

INNER BORDER

Orange:

Cut 4 strips 1½″ × WOF.

BINDING

Orange:

Cut 5 strips 2½″ × WOF.

PAPER-PIECED BLOCKS

Depending on whether you are a frugal paper-piecer or a generous paper-piecer, you might need to adjust the sizes given here for your rectangles. Make a sample block to test the size you prefer before cutting the pieces for the entire quilt. The sizes given here are generous sizes.

Orange:

Cut 28 strips 3″ × WOF; subcut 16 strips into 48 rectangles 3″ × 12″ and 12 strips into 48 rectangles 3″ × 9″.

> NOTE
>
> If your fabric is 42″ wide or wider, you will yield 4 rectangles 3″ × 9″ and 3 rectangles 3″ × 12″ from each strip.

Light gray:

Cut 30 strips 3″ × WOF; subcut 24 strips into 72 rectangles 3″ × 12″ and 6 strips into 24 rectangles 3″ × 9″.

Blocks

Use a ¼″ seam allowance. Refer to Basic Construction (page 8) as needed.

NINE-PATCHES

Using 5 orange and 4 light gray squares in each block, make 6 Nine-Patch blocks. *Fig. A*

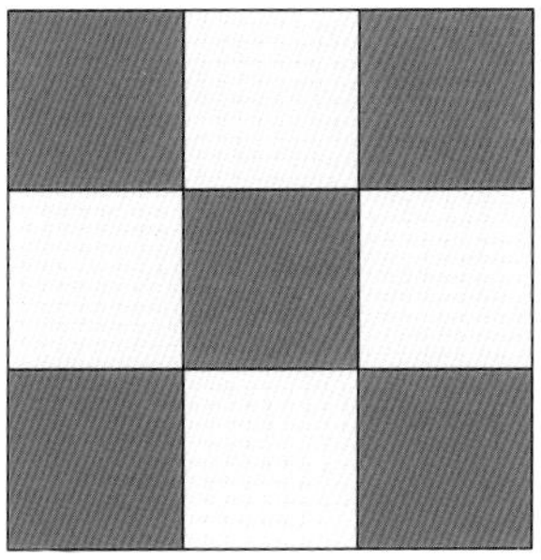

A 3½″ × 3½″

PAPER-PIECED UNITS

Using the *Starburst* pattern (page 48), prepare 24 units for paper piecing. Paper piece each unit using stitch-and-flip piecing.

STEP 1 Place a Color 1 and a Color 2 strip, right sides together, with the Color 1 strip on top. Place the paper pattern *printed side up* on top of the fabrics. Be sure the edges of the fabric extend at least ¼″ past the lines on the paper pattern. Pin.

STEP 2 Stitch along the stitching line between 1 and 2. *Fig. B*

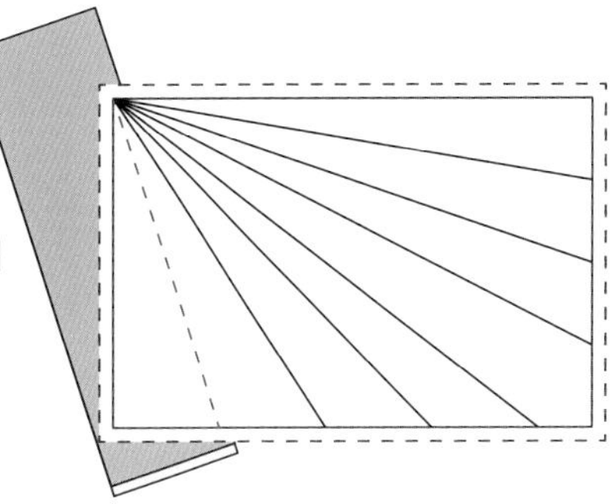

B

STEP 3 Turn the paper pattern over and fold it on the stitched line. Trim the seam allowance to ¼″. Turn the pattern over again and press the fabrics open. The right sides are visible. *Fig. C*

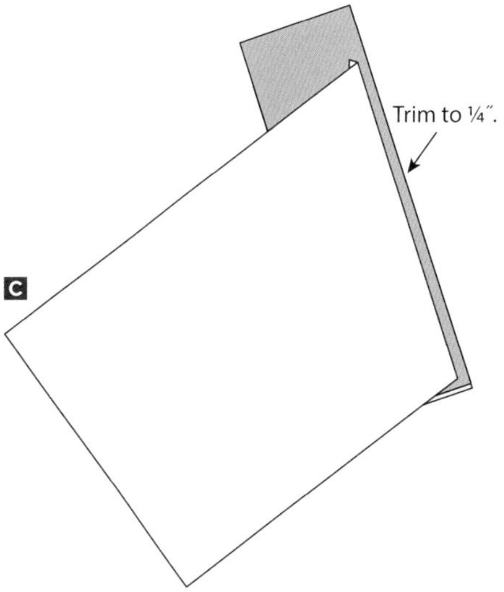

C

STEP 4 Turn the paper pattern over and fold the paper on the line between 2 and 3. Trim the excess fabric to ¼″. *Fig. D*

STEP 5 Open the paper pattern and trim off any extra strip length.

STEP 6 Turn the paper pattern over and place a Color 1 strip on top of the Color 2 strip, right sides together, matching the raw edge with the edge that was just trimmed. Pin.

STEP 7 Turn the paper pattern over and stitch along the stitching line between 2 and 3.

STEP 8 Continue adding strips, repeating Steps 3–7 to fill the paper pattern.

STEP 9 Trim each quarter-block to 6½″ × 9½″. Make 24. *Fig. E*

BLOCK ASSEMBLY

Using 4 paper-pieced units and 1 Nine-Patch unit each, make 6 blocks using partial seam piecing.

STEP 1 Place a Nine-Patch right sides together on top of a paper-pieced unit. The points of the paper-pieced unit should all touch the Nine-Patch at its corner. Sew from the outside edge to about halfway across the Nine-Patch. Backstitch and stop. There will be considerable bulk at the corners, so extra pinning may be required to avoid shifting. Press the sewn part of the seam toward the Nine-Patch. *Fig. F*

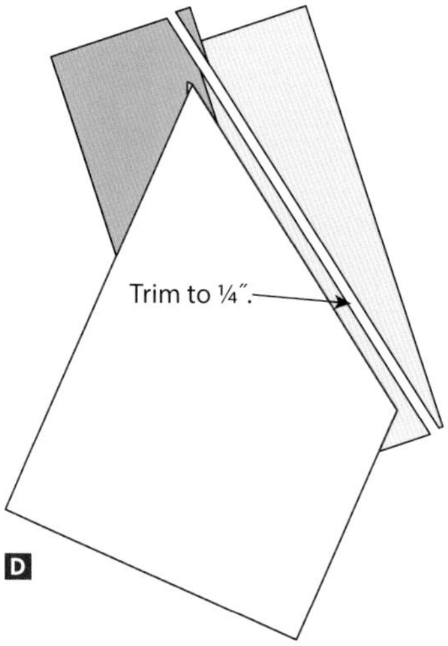

D

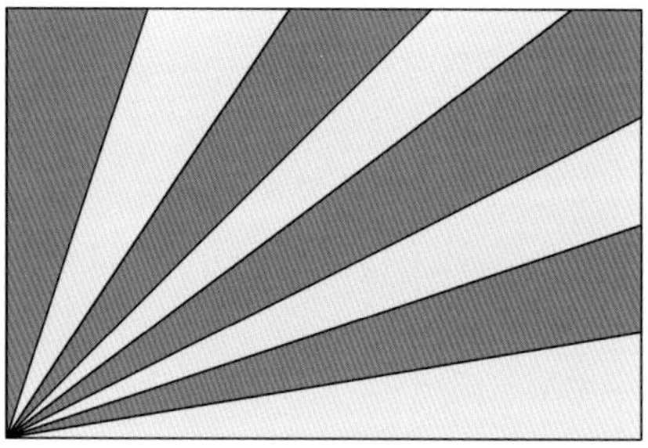
E 6½″ × 9½″

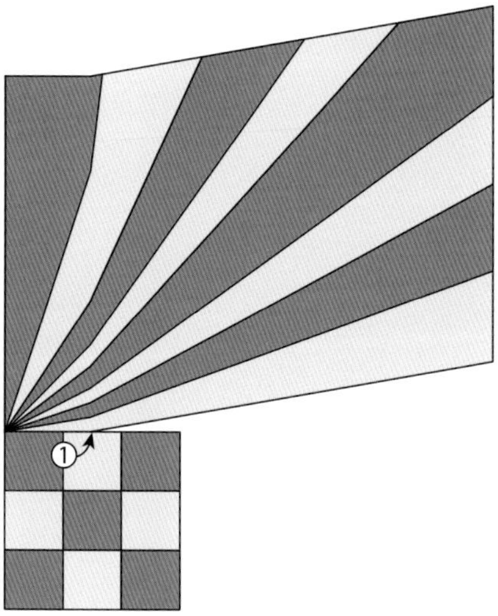

F

STEP 2 Place a second paper-pieced unit to the left side of the Step 1 unit, right sides together. Sew the entire length of the seam. Press toward the Nine-Patch. *Fig. G*

STEP 3 Continue around the Nine-Patch, repeating Step 2 for the third and fourth seams.

STEP 4 Finish the first seam. *Figs. H & I*

Assembly

Sew the blocks together in 3 rows of 2 each. Join the rows to complete the top center.

INNER BORDER

STEP 1 Sew the orange 1½″ × WOF strips together into 1 continuous strip.

STEP 2 Measure the quilt lengthwise from top to bottom through its middle and cut 2 strips to that length. They should be about 45½″ long.

STEP 3 Sew a strip to each side of the quilt. Press toward the border.

STEP 4 Repeat for the top and bottom borders. They should be about 32½″ long.

PIECED BORDER

STEP 1 Sew the 12 remaining orange and light gray 1½″ × WOF strips together lengthwise into 6 pairs. Subcut each into 1½″ strips to make 166 total 2-square units. *Fig. J*

STEP 2 Sew the 2-square units together checkerboard style in 4 strips for side, top, and bottom borders.

> NOTE
> Pay attention to how the checkerboard is pieced so the corners align perfectly.

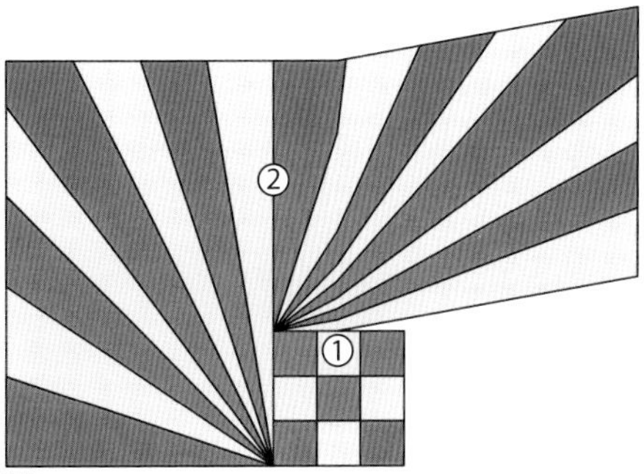

G

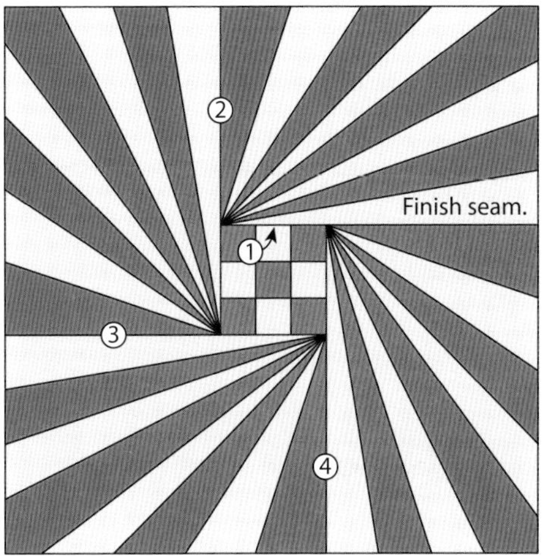

H

I 15½″ × 15½″

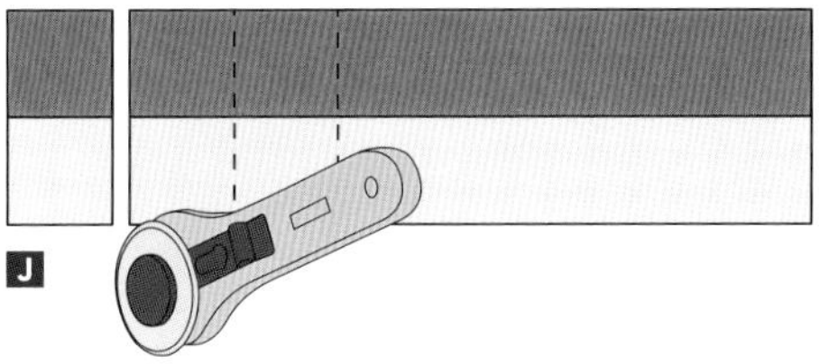
J

Side Borders

The side borders each have 47 units and start with a light gray square on the top left. Make 2. Sew a border to each side of the quilt and press toward the inner border. *Fig. K*

Top Border

The top border has 36 units and starts with a light gray square on the top left. Attach it to the top of the quilt and press toward the inner border. *Fig. L*

Bottom Border

The bottom border has 36 units and starts with an orange square on the top left. Sew it to the bottom and press to the inner border. *Fig. M*

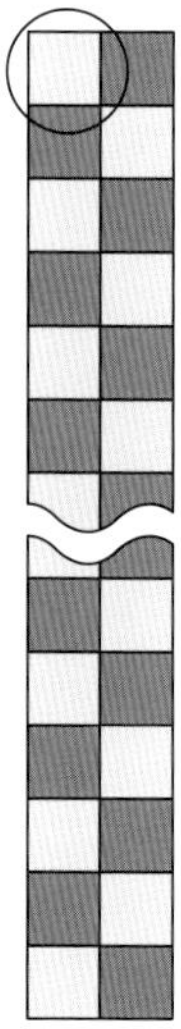
K

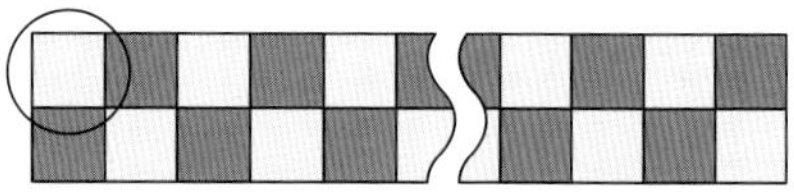
L

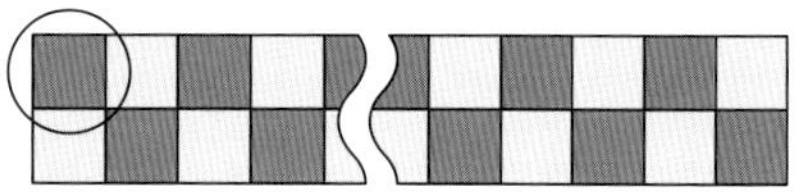
M

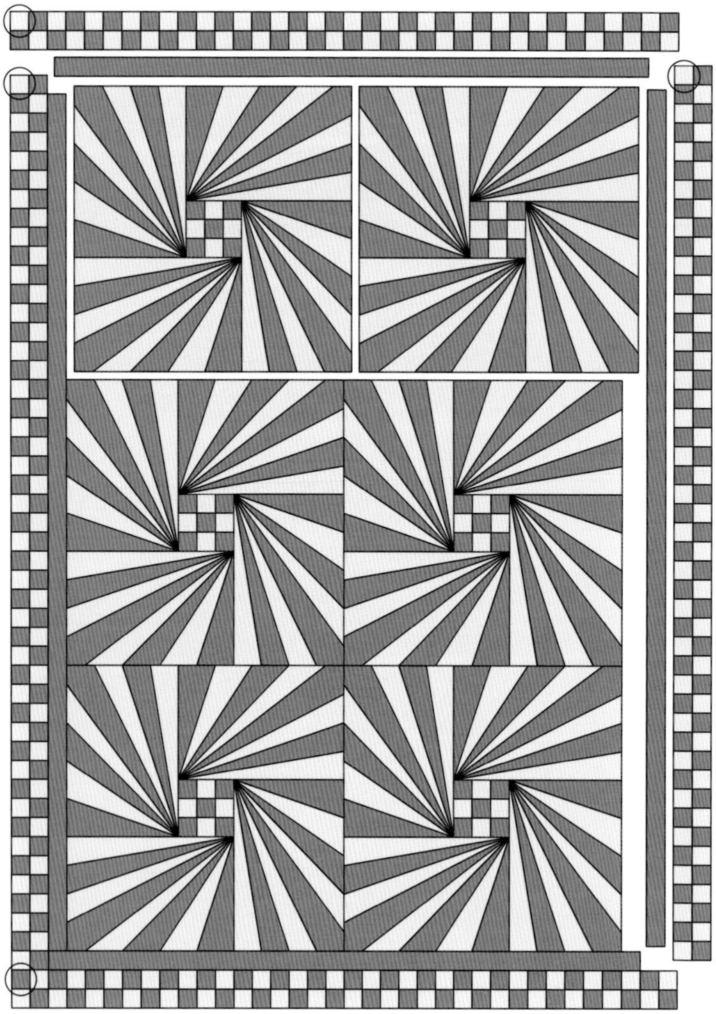
Quilt assembly

Finishing

Refer to Finishing the Quilt (page 12) as needed.

Layer and baste the quilt.

QUILTING

This beauty shows how radiant Nine-Patch blocks can be. Quilting straight lines to highlight the piecing is a great choice for such an intricate and beautiful design. It also shows that quilting doesn't have to be complex to be interesting.

Straight Lines

STEP 1 From the outer corner of the block, quilt a line that angles in towards the point of the wedge. Stop when there is about 1⁄4″ space on each side, and then angle back up toward the next seam. *Fig. N*

N

STEP 2 Repeat in the next wedge, ending at the next seam. *Fig. O*

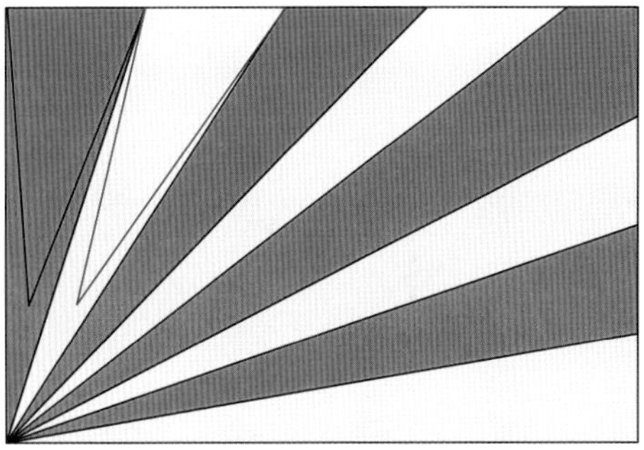

O

STEP 3 Continue in the rest of the wedges. *Fig. P*

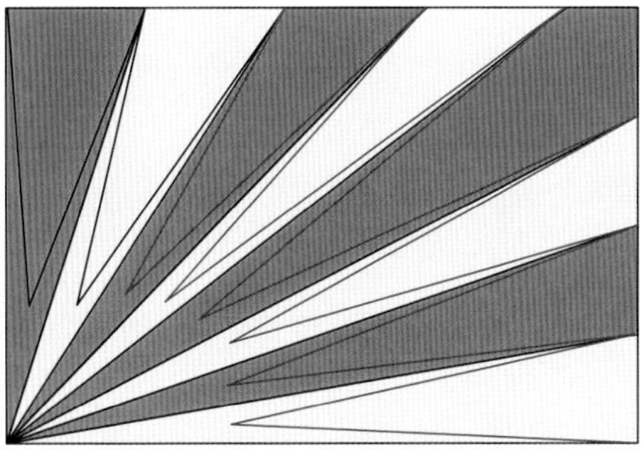

P

> NOTE
>
> Paper-pieced quilts tend to have bulky areas where several pieces of fabric come together. This design allows you to avoid those areas, hopefully preventing any broken needles while quilting.

THE LAST STEP

Add the binding to your quilt, referring to Binding (page 14) as needed. Note that *Starburst* requires about 190″ of binding.

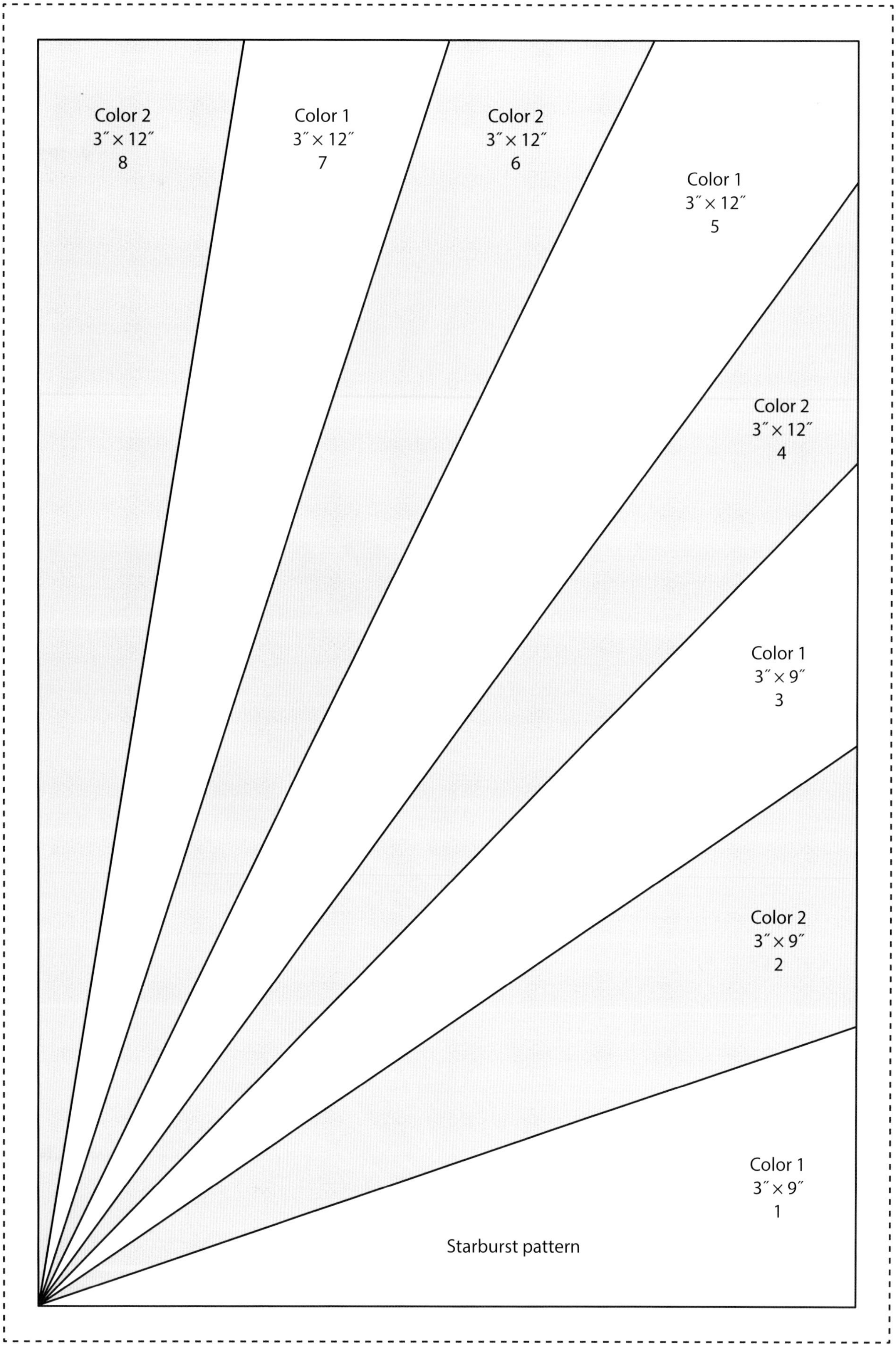

Starburst pattern

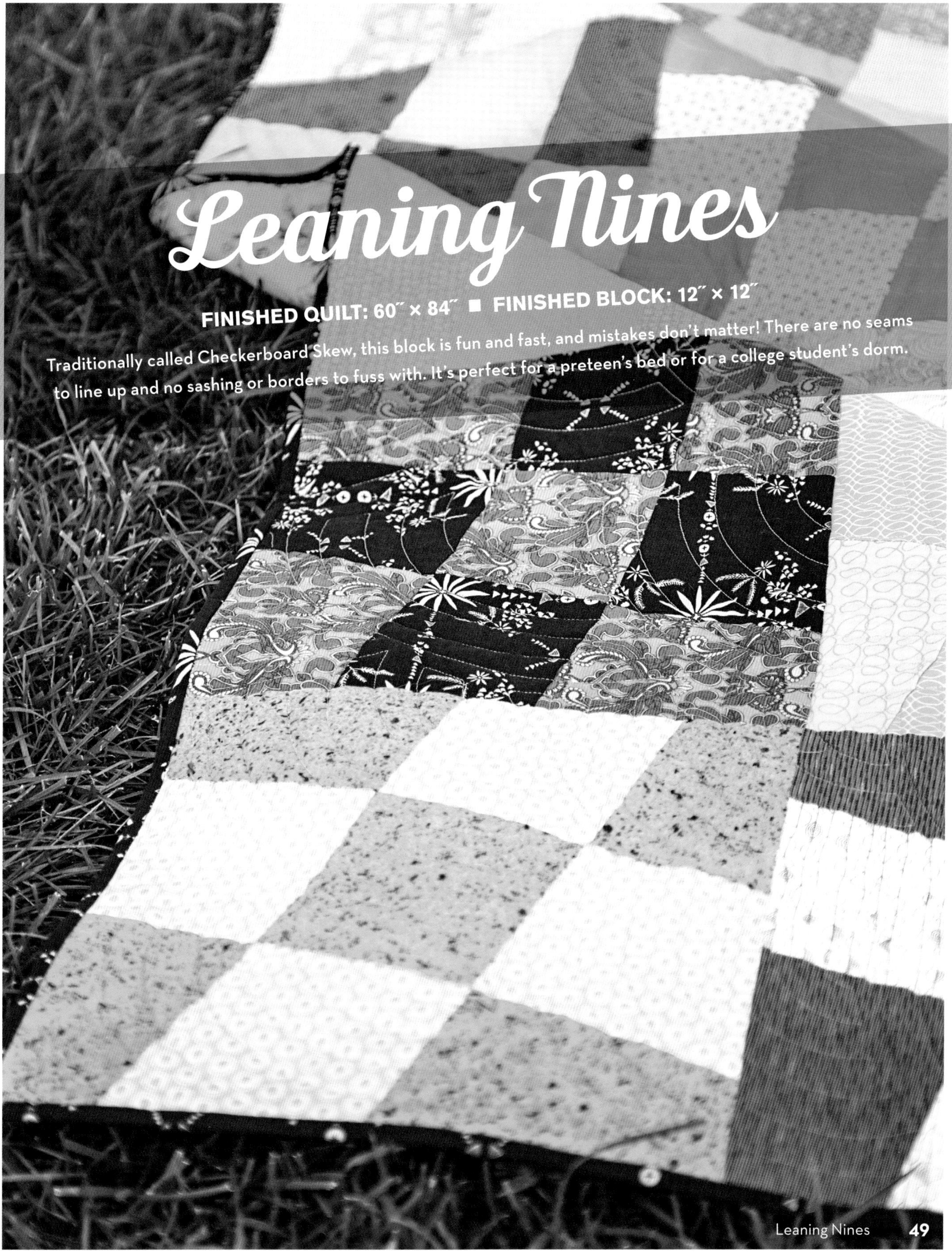

Leaning Nines

FINISHED QUILT: 60″ × 84″ ■ FINISHED BLOCK: 12″ × 12″

Traditionally called Checkerboard Skew, this block is fun and fast, and mistakes don't matter! There are no seams to line up and no sashing or borders to fuss with. It's perfect for a preteen's bed or for a college student's dorm.

Design Notes

Leaning Nines is made using a 70's color palette: orange, pink, lime green, aqua, and navy, and low volumes. Each fabric will be used in two blocks, so you need a maximum variety of prints and solids.

Fabrics

Yardage is based on 42″ usable fabric width. WOF = width of fabric.

Assorted fat quarters: 18 prints and 17 solids, or 25 prints and 10 solids

Binding: 5/8 yard coordinating print or solid

Backing: 5¼ yards coordinating print

Batting: 66″ × 90″

Cutting

FAT QUARTERS

Cut 35 squares 14″ × 14″.

BINDING

Cut 8 strips 2½″ × WOF.

Blocks

Use a ¼″ seam allowance. Refer to Basic Construction (page 8) as needed.

STEP 1 Stack 5 of the 14″ × 14″ squares on a cutting mat. Using a long ruler cut the stack in 2 vertical angles and 2 horizontal angles as shown. Work carefully so you don't disturb the stack as you cut. *Fig. A*

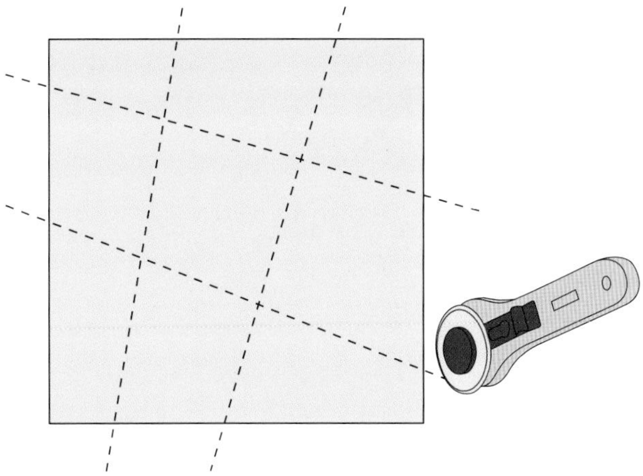

A Cutting

> NOTE
>
> By working in stacks of five, you'll get different angles as you cut, so not all the blocks will be identical.

STEP 2 After cutting, move the top 4 corner squares and the center square to the bottom of the pile in the same position. You now have 5 Nine-Patch blocks ready to sew. If you end up with a color combination you don't like, change it now.

STEP 3 Sew the Nine-Patches, and then trim each block to 12½″ × 12½″. Be careful of the bias edges. Stay stitch around the outer edges to prevent the blocks from distorting.

B 12½″ × 12½″

> NOTE
>
> When sewing, line up each piece edge to edge as if you were piecing a normal Nine-Patch. There is no need to offset the pieces to account for the angles.

STEP 4 Repeat with 6 more stacks of 5 squares to make 35 blocks total. *Fig. B*

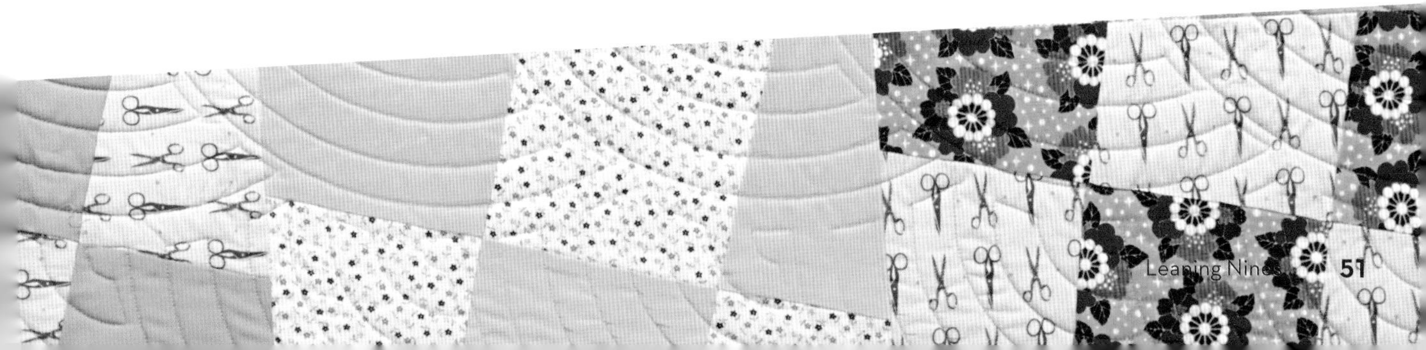

Assembly

Lay out the blocks in 7 rows of 5 blocks each. Make sure the color distribution is pleasing to your eye. Sew them together in rows, and then join the rows.

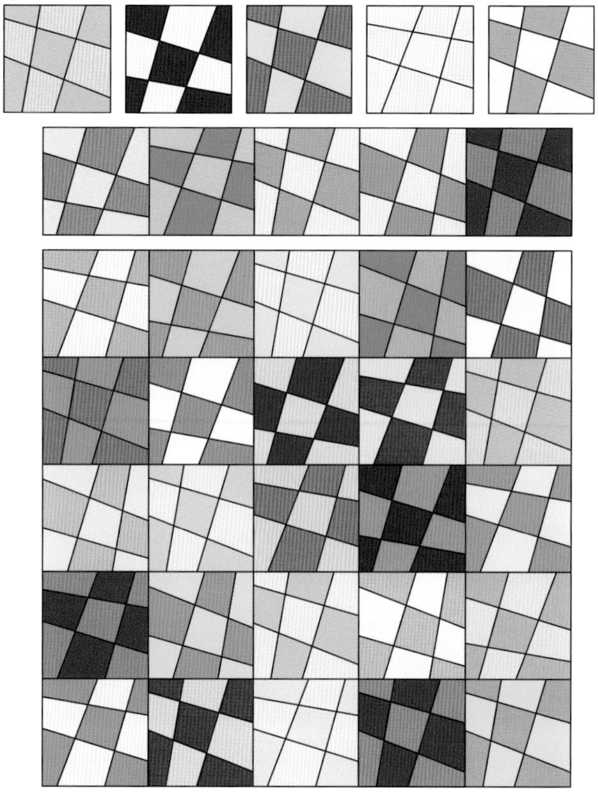

Quilt assembly

Finishing

Refer to Finishing the Quilt (page 12) as needed.

Layer and baste the quilt.

QUILTING

Some quilt tops are just perfect for an allover design, and this is one of them. The scrappy layout of the quilt and the fun wonkiness of the blocks mean that the quilting won't be too noticeable. This can be nice when you're trying out a new quilting design or just want to finish the quilt quickly.

Any allover quilting design works in this quilt. The Baptist Fan quilting design, with its nostalgia of days past, is a great option. Even if the lines aren't perfect, it won't be noticeable. However, if you are more of a perfectionist, use a stencil to get those fans lined up just right.

THE LAST STEP

Add the binding to your quilt, referring to Binding (page 14) as needed. Note that *Leaning Nines* requires about 300″ of binding.

Controlled Chaos

FINISHED QUILT: 60″ × 90″ ■ FINISHED BLOCK: 3″ × 6″

In the midst of chaos, there is a plan to this quilt! Colored solids and prints intermingle as Nine-Patches with five gradating grays consistently flow from top to bottom. The prints are the chaos but the solids are the control, giving structure and a place for your eye to grab on to and rest.

Design Notes

While 200 blocks can be daunting, it's easy to make this quilt over time using Bonnie Hunter's "Leaders and Enders" technique. Keep the solid sets and prints next to your machine and, as you piece other quilts, sew the units a few at a time in between sewing other blocks. When you're ready to finish, you won't have so many blocks to complete at once!

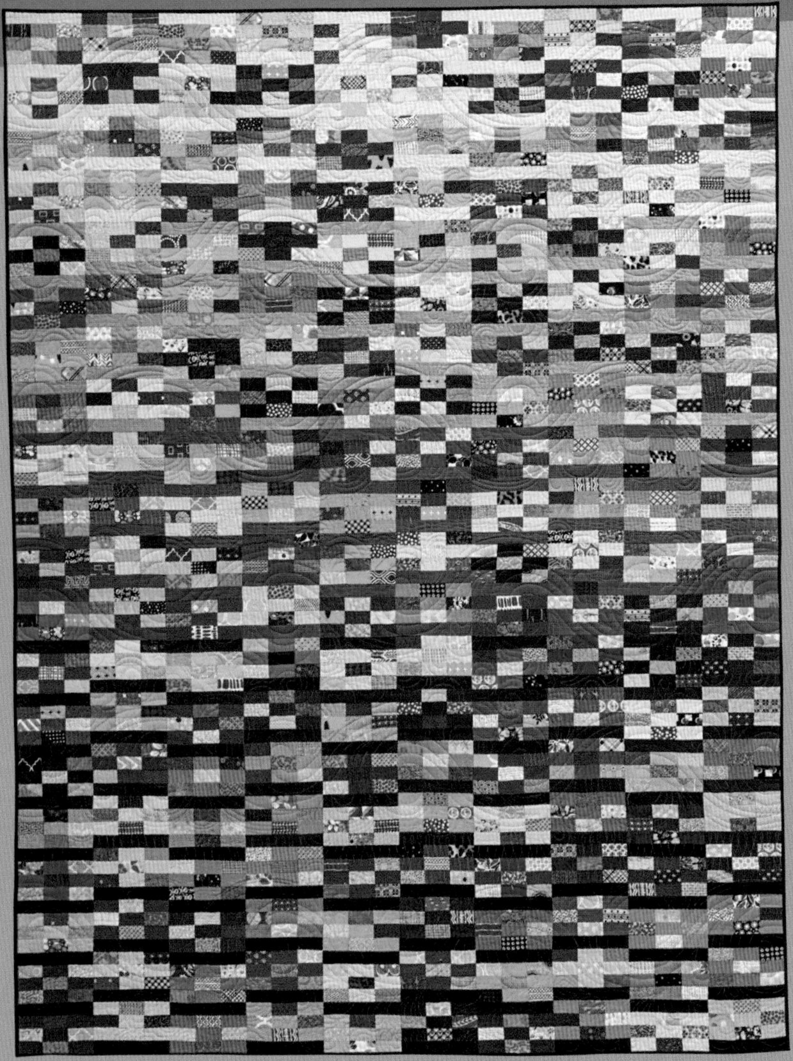

Fabrics

Yardage is based on 42″ usable fabric width. WOF = width of fabric.

Gray solids: ⅓ yard each of 5 solids, in a 5-step gradation from light gray to black

Assorted prints: Large collection of scraps in all colors of the rainbow—*the more variety, the more interesting the quilt.* Suggestions: You may use either 22–25 fat eighths, 150–160 squares 5″ × 5″ (4 precut packs), or 38–42 squares 10″ × 10″ (1 precut pack).

Assorted solids: You may use either 150–160 scraps (at least 5″ × 5″ each), 22–25 fat eighths, or 10–12 fat quarters.

Dark print or solid: ⅝ yard for binding

Coordinating print: 5½ yards for backing

Batting: 66″ × 96″

Cutting

GRAY GRADATION SOLIDS

From each solid:

Cut 7 strips 1½″ × WOF; subcut 40 rectangles 1½″ × 6½″.

ASSORTED SCRAPS OR OTHER CUTS

Solids:

Cut 100 sets of 4 matching rectangles 1½″ × 2½″.

Cut 100 sets of 5 matching rectangles 1½″ × 2½″.

Prints:

Cut 900 rectangles 1½″ × 2½″.

BINDING

Cut 8 strips 2½″ × WOF.

Blocks

Use a ¼″ seam allowance. Refer to Basic Construction (page 8) as needed.

The quilt consists of 100 Nine-Patch blocks with matching solids on the corners (Block A) and 100 Nine-Patch blocks with random prints on the corners (Block B).

> NOTE
> Each block has matching solids, but the prints are random—don't worry about matching the prints by color or organizing them in any other way. Remember, the solids are the control and the prints are the chaos.

BLOCK A

Using 5 matching solids and 4 random prints in each block, make 100 Block A's. Press the seams *open.*

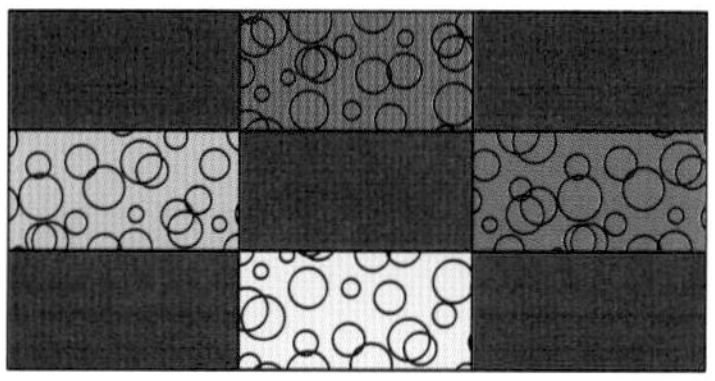

3½″ × 6½″

BLOCK B

Using 4 matching solids and 5 random prints in each block, make 100 Block B's. Press the seams *open.*

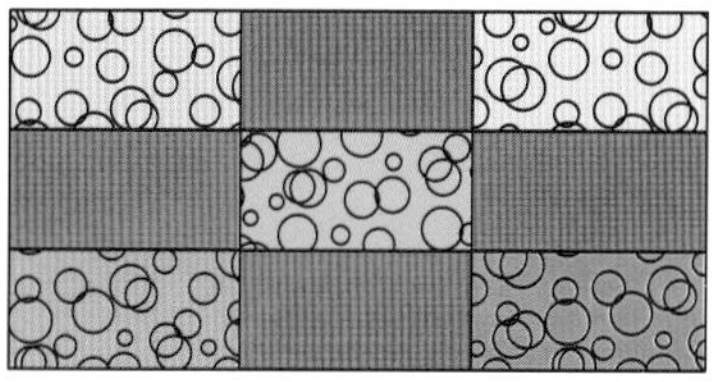

3½″ × 6½″

> NOTE
> Pressing the seams open makes it easier to match seams perfectly when joining the blocks.

Sashing

Sew the gray rectangles to the blocks, making sure to match 20 of each gray to 20 Block A's and the remaining 20 of each gray to 20 Block B's. Press the seams open.

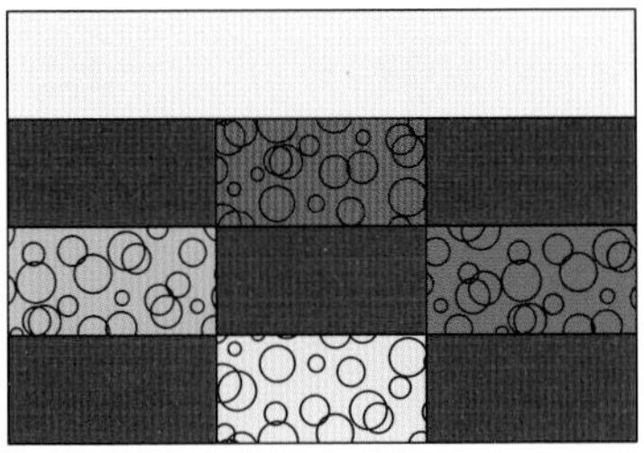

Block A with sashing

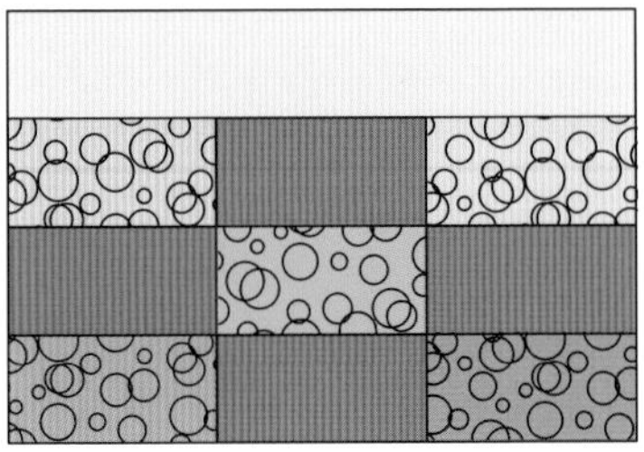

Block B with sashing

> **NOTE**
>
> Organization is important at this point. As you finish piecing the sashing to the blocks keep the blocks in separate piles by sashing color. Place the lightest gray in 2 stacks: 1 stack of Block A with light gray sashing and 1 stack of Block B with light gray sashing. Repeat with the remaining 4 grays so you end up with 10 stacks when you finish piecing the sashing to the blocks. The blocks now measure 4½″ × 6½″.

Assembly

The quilt is made of 20 rows of 10 blocks each. The rows alternate, starting with Block B in row 1, Block A in row 2, Block B in row 3, and so on. The sashing gradates from top to bottom with the lightest at the top of the quilt.

To stay organized, it's easiest to work in panels rather than rows. Each panel is made of 20 blocks: 10 Block A's and 10 Block B's.

PANELS

Left Panel

From the blocks with the light gray sashing, choose 10 Block A's and 10 Block B's. Pay attention to the color of the solids so you don't end up with too many of the same solid colors close to each other. Sometimes this is unavoidable, and that's okay!

For the left panel, always start with Block B sashing above in the upper left corner. Lay out 5 Block B's as shown, alternating the sashing above and below. Sew them together in a row and press the seams open.

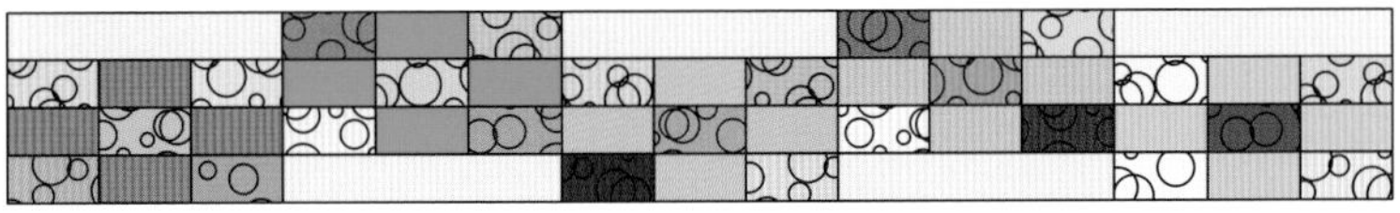

Block B, rows 1 and 3

Block A, rows 2 and 4

Make 2 rows of 10 Block B's and 2 rows of 10 Block A's per panel. Join the 4 rows together.

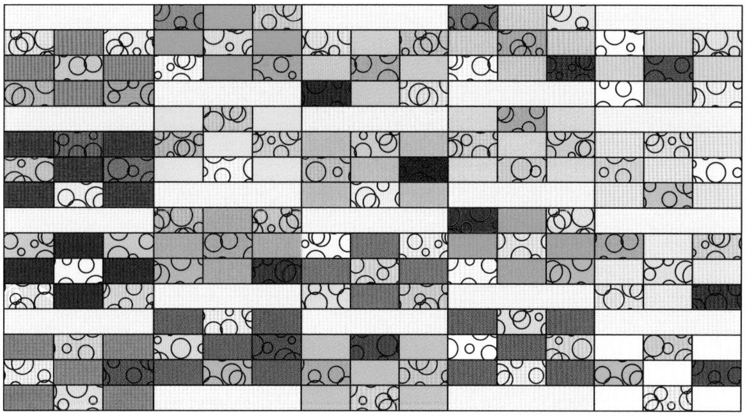

Left panel

Right Panel

Use the remaining 20 light gray Block A's and 20 light gray Block B's to make the right panel.

Start with the Block B in the upper left corner *but this time* the sashing is below. Lay out 5 Block B's as shown, alternating the sashing below and above. Sew them together in a row and press the seams open.

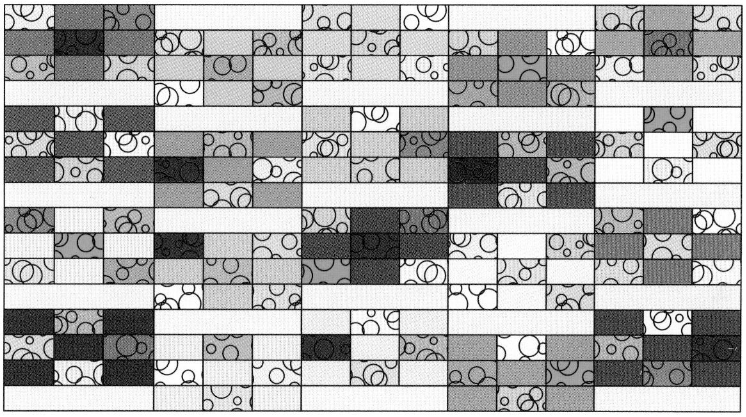

Right panel

PANEL ASSEMBLY

Place the 2 panels side by side, making sure the left panel has Block B light gray sashing above in the top left corner and the right panel has Block B sashing below in the top left position. Sew the 2 panels together, and press the seams open.

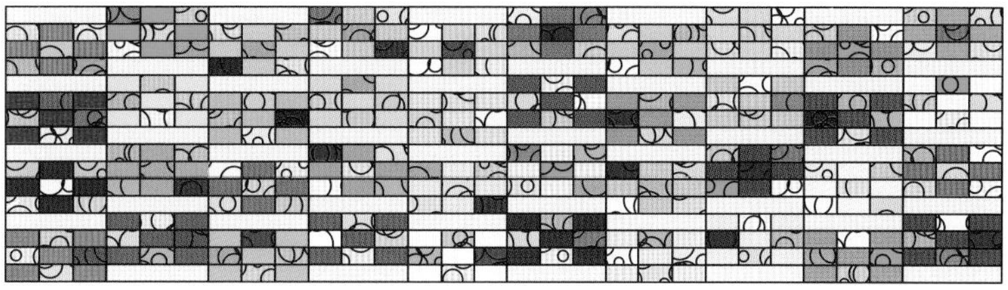

Repeat with the remaining 4 gradated sashing colors to make 10 panels of 20 blocks each. Join the 5 sections.

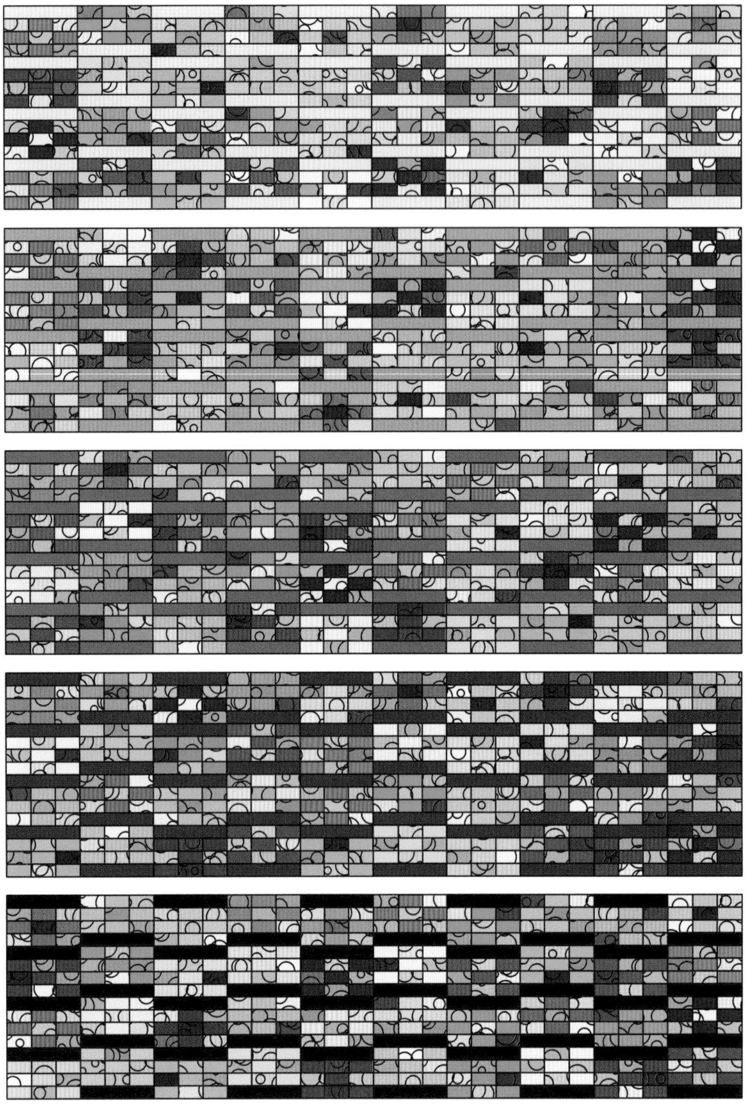

Quilt assembly

Finishing

Refer to Finishing the Quilt (page 12) as needed.

Layer and baste the quilt.

QUILTING

Sometimes using the quilting to fit the blocks is a great way to finish a quilt. Other times, you may wish to quilt a design that disregards the blocks altogether. *Controlled Chaos* can be quilted either way, but you might find that you like the freedom of forgetting the piecing when quilting.

To try this option, quilt a design, such as elongated swirls, in rows spaced out from each other. Leaving 4″–5″ between the rows gives you room to use some of your favorite fillers.

If you like the look of quilting with a similar allover texture, you can fill in between the rows with more swirls.

Quilting similar designs provides similar texture throughout quilt

To make the rows of swirls stand out from each other, you can use a filler, such as the wishbone design. It is different enough from the swirls so that they don't blend into each other.

Quilting a different design helps swirls stand out.

Wishbone Design

While the wishbone design might not be the first thing you think of when picking filler designs, it's a great one to use. It is quick to quilt and can fill irregularly shaped areas, such as the space between rows of swirls.

STEP 1 Starting from one side of the area, quilt a line that angles down toward the opposite side. As you approach the opposite side, loop back in the direction you came from and angle back toward the first side. *Fig. A*

STEP 2 As you approach the first side, loop around and angle toward the opposite side. *Fig. B*

> NOTE
>
> If the sides are irregularly shaped or uneven, simply extend the line until you are close the edge. It doesn't matter if the length of the wishbones vary, just make sure that the whole area is filled in as completely as possible.

STEP 3 Begin the next line, trying to quilt it parallel to the previously quilted one. *Fig. C*

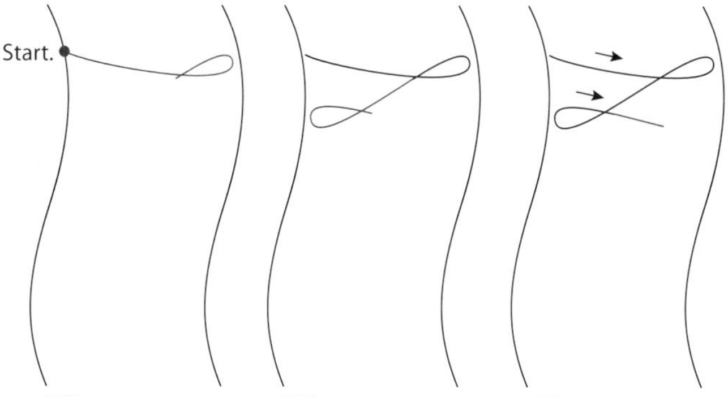

A B C

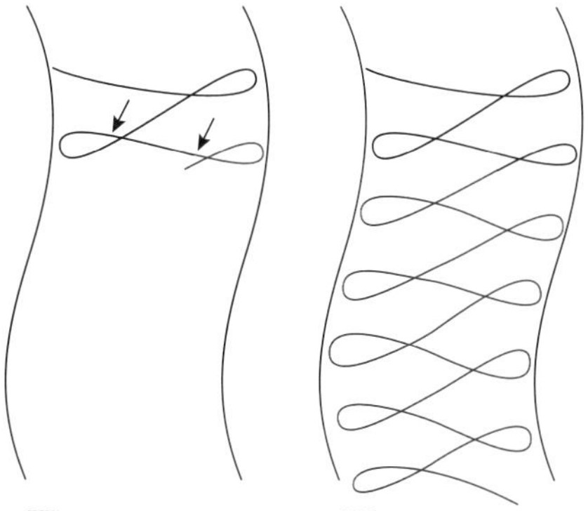

D E

> NOTE
>
> Keeping the lines parallel helps ensure that the design progresses in the right direction. Don't worry about making it any particular angle, just focus on getting it somewhat parallel.

STEP 4 Repeat by quilting the next line in the opposite direction, keeping it parallel to the other line going the same direction. *Fig. D*

STEP 5 Continue quilting until the space is filled. *Fig. E*

THE LAST STEP

Add the binding to your quilt, referring to Binding (page 14) as needed. Note that *Controlled Chaos* requires about 320″ of binding.

Nine-Patch Surround

FINISHED QUILT: 60″ × 72″ ■ FINISHED BLOCK: 6″ × 6″

Nine-Patch Surround is a scrap quilt with endless possibilities. Using solids from the lightest of lights to the darkest of darks in all colors of the rainbow makes a pleasing pixilated quilt.

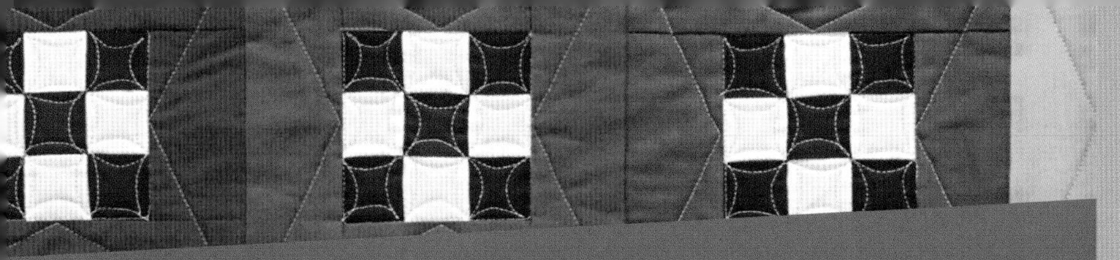

Design Notes

Once the blocks are made, go crazy with experimentation! Group together by color as shown, group by value regardless of color, or mix everything up randomly. Your favorite version will present itself and you'll have a one-of-a-kind rainbow quilt.

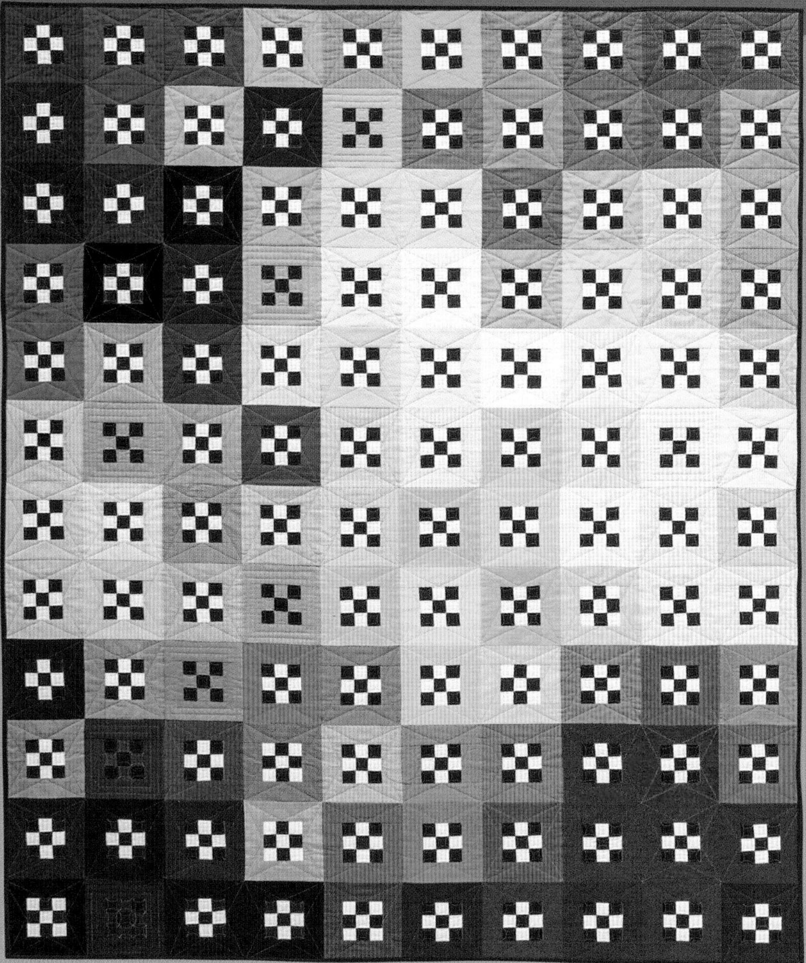

Fabrics

Yardage is based on 42″ usable fabric width. WOF = width of fabric.

Charcoal gray: 1⅛ yards

White: ⅞ yard

Assorted solids: Up to 120 different solids in all colors of the rainbow (plus gray): 8″ × 8″ scraps or fat eighths of each color. *If repeating colors, keep repeats to a minimum.*

Dark gray solid: ⅝ yard for binding

Coordinating print: 3⅞ yards for backing

Batting: 66″ × 78″

Cutting

CHARCOAL GRAY

Cut 25 strips 1½″ × WOF.

WHITE

Cut 20 strips 1½″ × WOF.

ASSORTED SOLIDS

For each block's solid surround (120 sets):

Cut 2 rectangles 2″ × 6½″.

Cut 2 rectangles 2″ × 3½″.

BINDING

Cut 8 strips 2½″ × WOF.

Blocks

Use a ¼″ seam allowance. Refer to Strip-Set Construction (page 11) as needed.

NINE-PATCH BLOCKS

STEP 1 Using 20 charcoal gray 1½″ × WOF strips and 10 white 1½″ × WOF strips, make 10 charcoal / white / charcoal strip sets. Cross-cut a total of 240 segments 1½″ wide.

STEP 2 Using 10 white 1½″ × WOF strips and 5 charcoal gray 1½″ × WOF strips, make an additional 5 white / charcoal / white strip sets. Cross-cut a total of 120 segments 1½″ wide.

STEP 3 Using 2 segments from Step 1 and 1 segment from Step 2, piece together the blocks. Make 120 Nine-Patches.

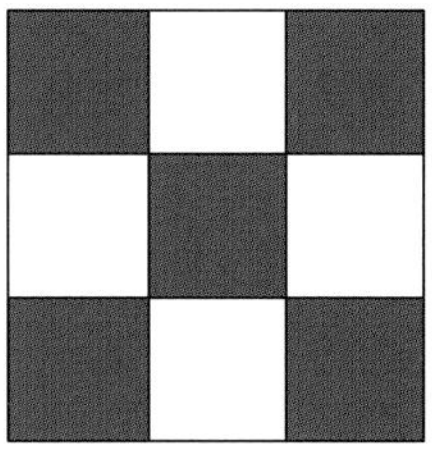

3½″ × 3½″

SURROUND

Use a set of solid block surround rectangles and 1 Nine-Patch. Sew the shorter 2″ × 3½″ rectangles to the sides of the Nine-Patch. Press toward the solid rectangles. Sew the longer 2″ × 6½″ rectangles to the top and bottom. Make 120 different colored blocks.

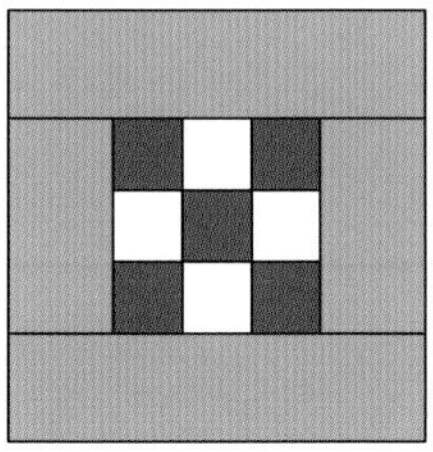

6½″ × 6½″

Assembly

Lay out the 120 blocks in 12 rows of 10 blocks each. Sew them together in rows, then join the rows.

> NOTE
>
> Stand back or take a picture on your phone to get a true picture of the way the quilt will look.

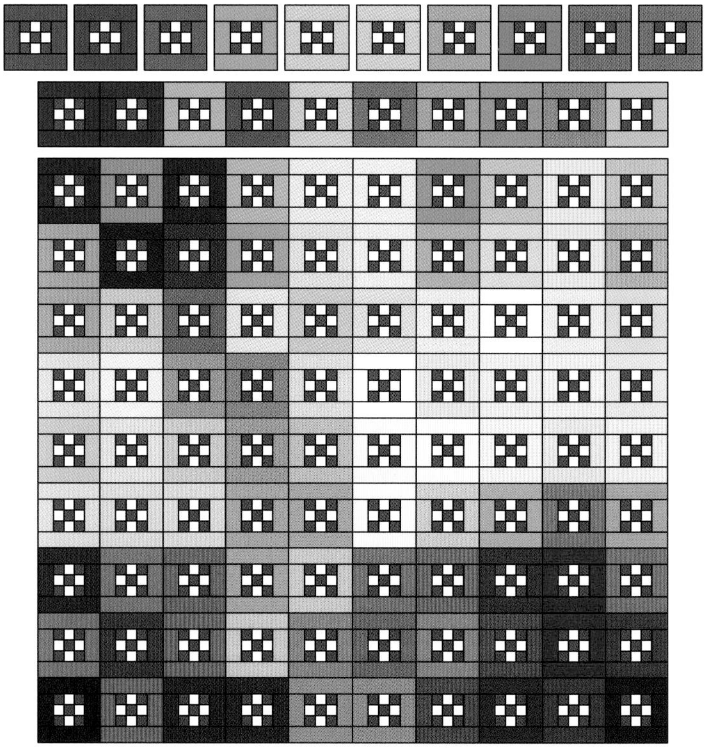

Quilt assembly

Finishing

Refer to Finishing the Quilt (page 12) as needed.

Layer and baste the quilt.

QUILTING

Just like a picture frame, the borders make the Nine-Patch blocks in the center shine. This kind of quilting draws attention to the piecing and creates secondary designs. The best part: It's easy!

Nine-Patch Rays

STEP 1 Starting on the outer corner of the block, quilt a diagonal line to the center of the top of the Nine-Patch. Quilt another diagonal line to the next corner of the block. *Fig. A*

STEP 2 Repeat on the next 2 sides. Quilt half of the last side, stopping when you reach the Nine-Patch. *Fig. B*

STEP 3 Stitch along the seams of the Nine-Patch, stopping at the lower left hand corner of the Nine-Patch. *Fig. C*

STEP 4 Quilt the Nine-Patch with continuous curves (page 13), returning to the same corner of the Nine-Patch. *Fig. D*

STEP 5 Finish stitching-in-the-ditch, then quilt a diagonal line to the starting point in Step 1. *Fig. E*

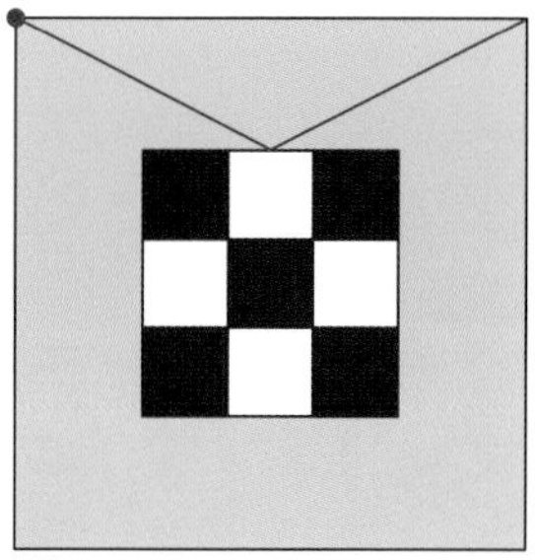

A

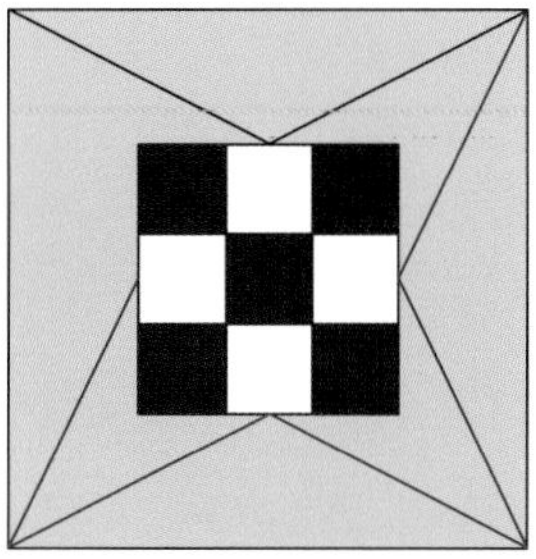

B

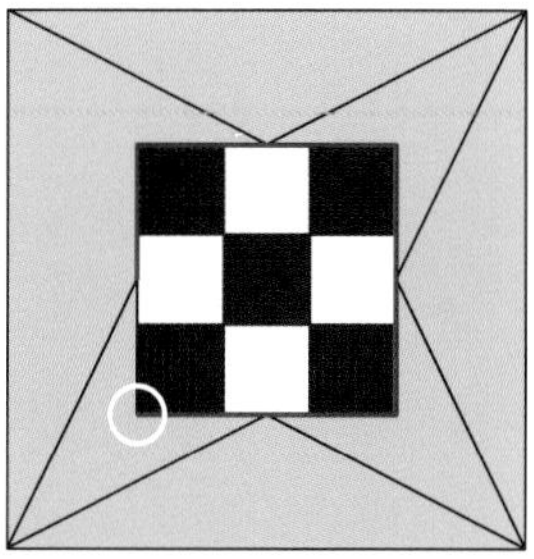

C

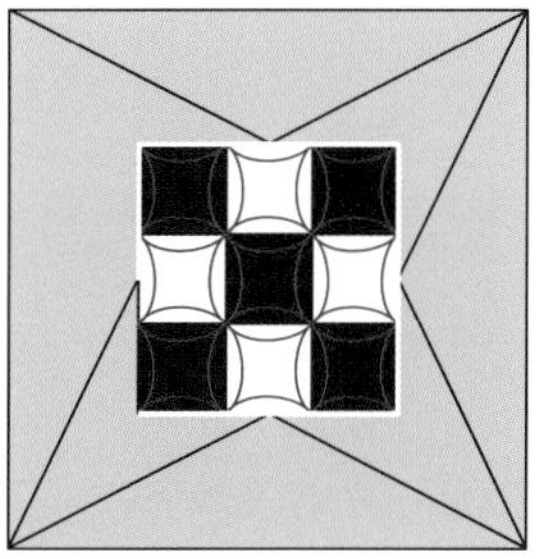

D

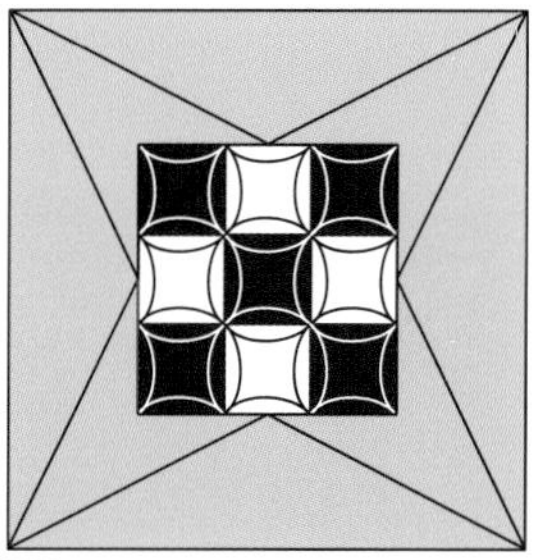

E

Do you want a simpler quilting option? Quilt echo lines around the block. It's easy to do and still emphasizes the center of the block.

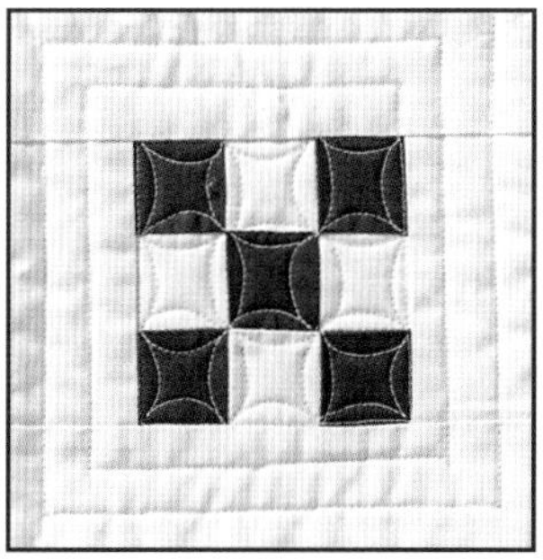

THE LAST STEP

Add the binding to your quilt, referring to Binding (page 14) as needed. Note that *Nine-Patch Surround* requires about 280″ of binding.

Streaked Lightning

FINISHED QUILT: 63″ × 72″ ■ FINISHED BLOCK: 9″ × 9″

Streak of Lightning is the name of an old-fashioned setting for Log Cabin blocks, named for the lightning effect that appears across the quilt when the blocks are set together. The lightning in *Streaked Lightning* appears when improv-pieced accents are set reminiscent of those old quilts.

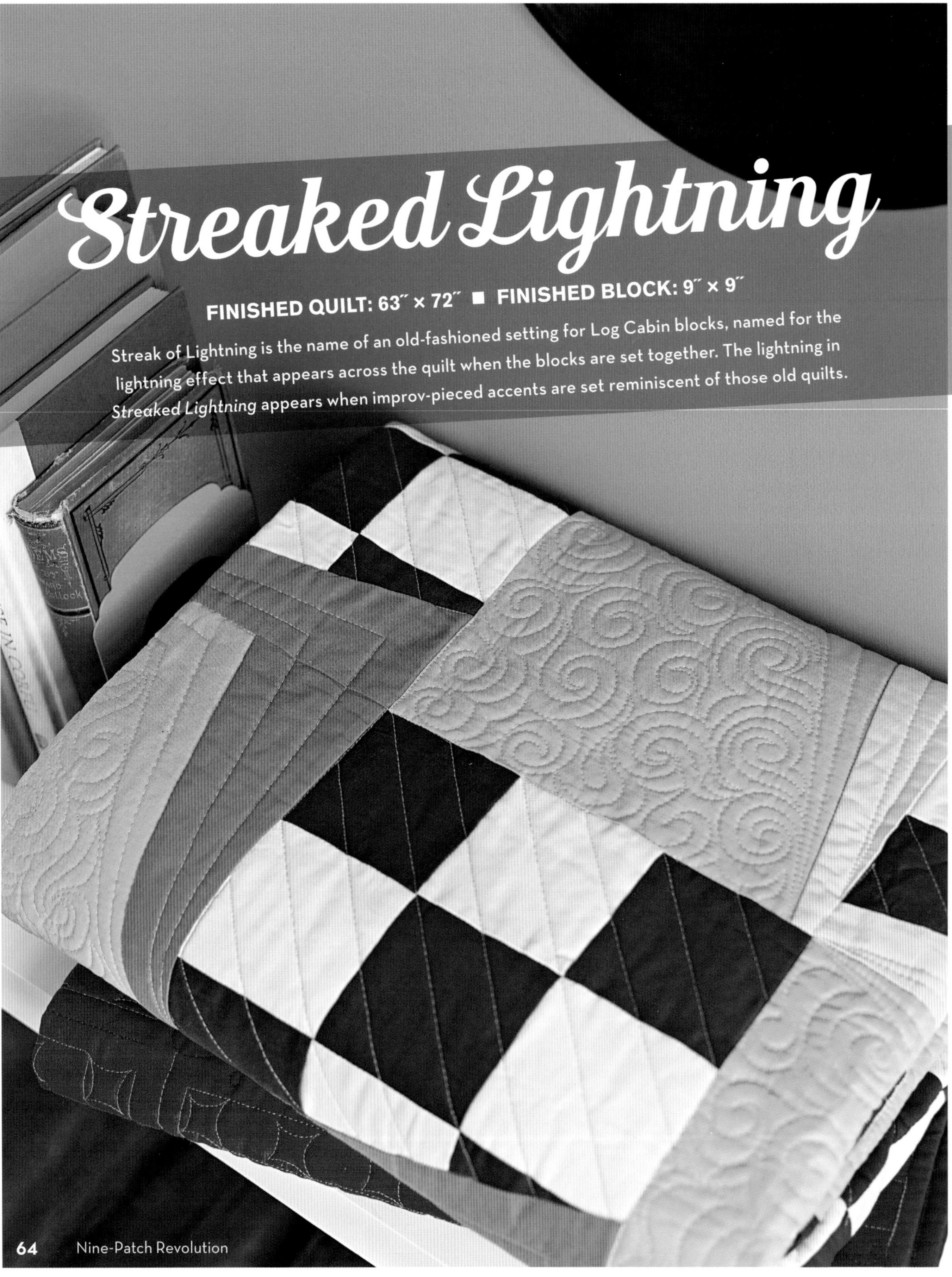

Design Notes

You can alternate each Nine-Patch block with any color you choose as long as the lighting accents pop off it.

Fabrics

Yardage is based on 42″ usable fabric width. WOF = width of fabric.

Blue solid: 2⅛ yards

Dark gray solid: 2 yards (1⅜ yards for blocks, ⅝ yard for binding)

Light gray solid: 1¼ yards

Accent solids:

- **Red:** ½ yard
- **Orange:** ½ yard
- **Gold:** ¼ yard
- **Cream:** 1 fat quarter

Blue solid: 4 yards for backing

Batting: 69″ × 78″

Cutting

BLUE

Cut 7 strips 9½″ × WOF; subcut 28 squares 9½″ × 9½″.

DARK GRAY

Cut 13 strips 3½″ × WOF.

LIGHT GRAY

Cut 11 strips 3½″ × WOF.

ACCENT SOLIDS

These will be cut as you go, improv-style.

BINDING

Cut 7 strips 2½″ × WOF.

Blocks

Use a 1/4″ seam allowance. Refer to Strip-Set Construction (page 11) as needed.

STEP 1 Using 10 dark gray 3½″ × WOF strips and 5 light gray 3½″ × WOF strips, make 5 strip sets, dark / light / dark.

STEP 2 Using 6 light gray strips and 3 dark gray strips, make 3 strip sets, light / dark / light.

STEP 3 Cross-cut all strip sets into 3½″ units. Use 2 units from Step 1 and 1 unit from Step 2 to make a Nine-Patch. Make 28 blocks. *Fig. A*

A 9½″ × 9½″

Block Accents

An accent piece is sewn to one side of each Nine-Patch block and blue alternate block. This is done improv-style, so precision is not necessary.

STEP 1 From an accent color, cut a large rectangle, and then cut it in half lengthwise on an angle for 2 accent pieces. Make sure the rectangle is oversized so the block trims to 9½″ × 9½″. For your "large rectangle," I recommend a width of 10½″; as for the height, a good rule of thumb is to make it about one-third the size of the finished block. Try one rectangle first before cutting all the fabric. For guidance, refer to the project photo (page 65). *Fig. B*

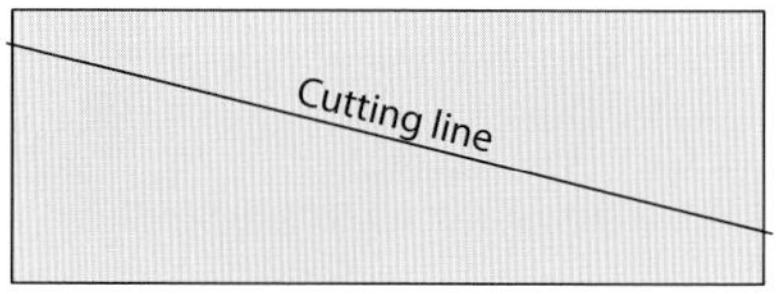

B

STEP 2 Try adding an accent piece to a Nine-Patch before proceeding. Sew the accent to one side of the block. Flip back and press. Trim to 9½″ × 9½″. *Figs. C–E*

C

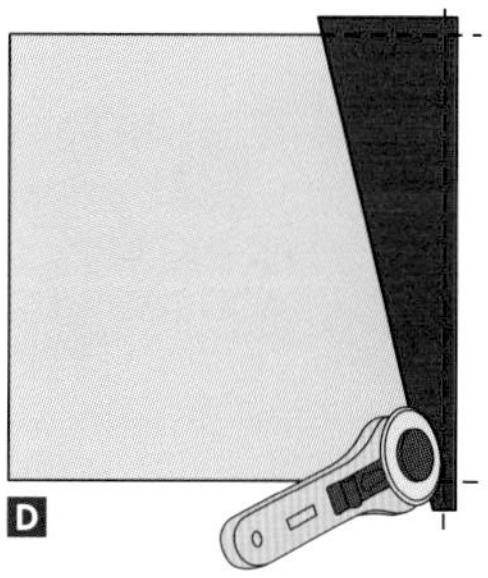

D

STEP 3 When you are sure of the size to cut the accent triangle, proceed with the rest. Eyeball the cutting of the rectangles so each one is different.

Cut the following from each accent solid:

Cream: 3 rectangles to accent 3 Nine-Patches and 3 solid blocks

Gold: 7 rectangles to accent 7 Nine-Patches and 7 solid blocks

Orange: 11 rectangles to accent 11 Nine-Patches and 11 solid blocks

Red: 7 rectangles to accent 7 Nine-Patches and 7 solid blocks

E

Assembly

STEP 1 Lay out the blocks in 8 rows of 7 blocks each, making sure to alternate blocks and Nine-Patches every other one. To achieve the lightning effect, the accent color should always be turned to the right side of the alternate blocks and to the bottom of the Nine-Patches.

STEP 2 Sew the blocks together in rows, then join the rows.

Quilt assembly

Finishing

Refer to Finishing the Quilt (page 12) as needed.

Layer and baste the quilt.

QUILTING

Even though this quilt is pieced row by row, the overall effect has a more diagonal look.

Using those diagonal lines as inspiration for quilting the blocks can help the quilting enhance the design. It's also a bonus that the pieces of the block can be used as a guide to keep the lines spaced evenly.

You can even extend the "theme" of quilting to the accent pieces of the blocks by quilting diagonal lines in those blocks as well.

In the Blocks

STEP 1 Starting about 1″ above the bottom left corner, quilt a diagonal line until you reach the seam of the accent block. Travel along the seam about 1″. *Fig. A*

> NOTE
>
> While traveling along the seam means more quilting, it also means that you won't have to break the thread to start a new line of quilting. If you don't like traveling, you can cut the threads and start a new line of quilting.

STEP 2 Echo the line you just quilted back to the edge of the block. *Fig. B*

STEP 3 Travel along the seam and repeat the process. *Fig. C*

STEP 4 Continue quilting echo lines and traveling until the entire block is quilted. *Fig. D*

A

B

C

D

THE LAST STEP

Add the binding to your quilt, referring to Binding (page 14) as needed. Note that *Streaked Lightning* requires about 285″ of binding.

Fraternal Twins

FINISHED QUILT: 63″ × 93″ ■ FINISHED BLOCK: 9″ × 9″

These *Fraternal Twins* quilts are almost the same but so different. The blocks are identical but the setting makes them look inversed! Easy setting squares and sashing make the two go together in just under eight hours!

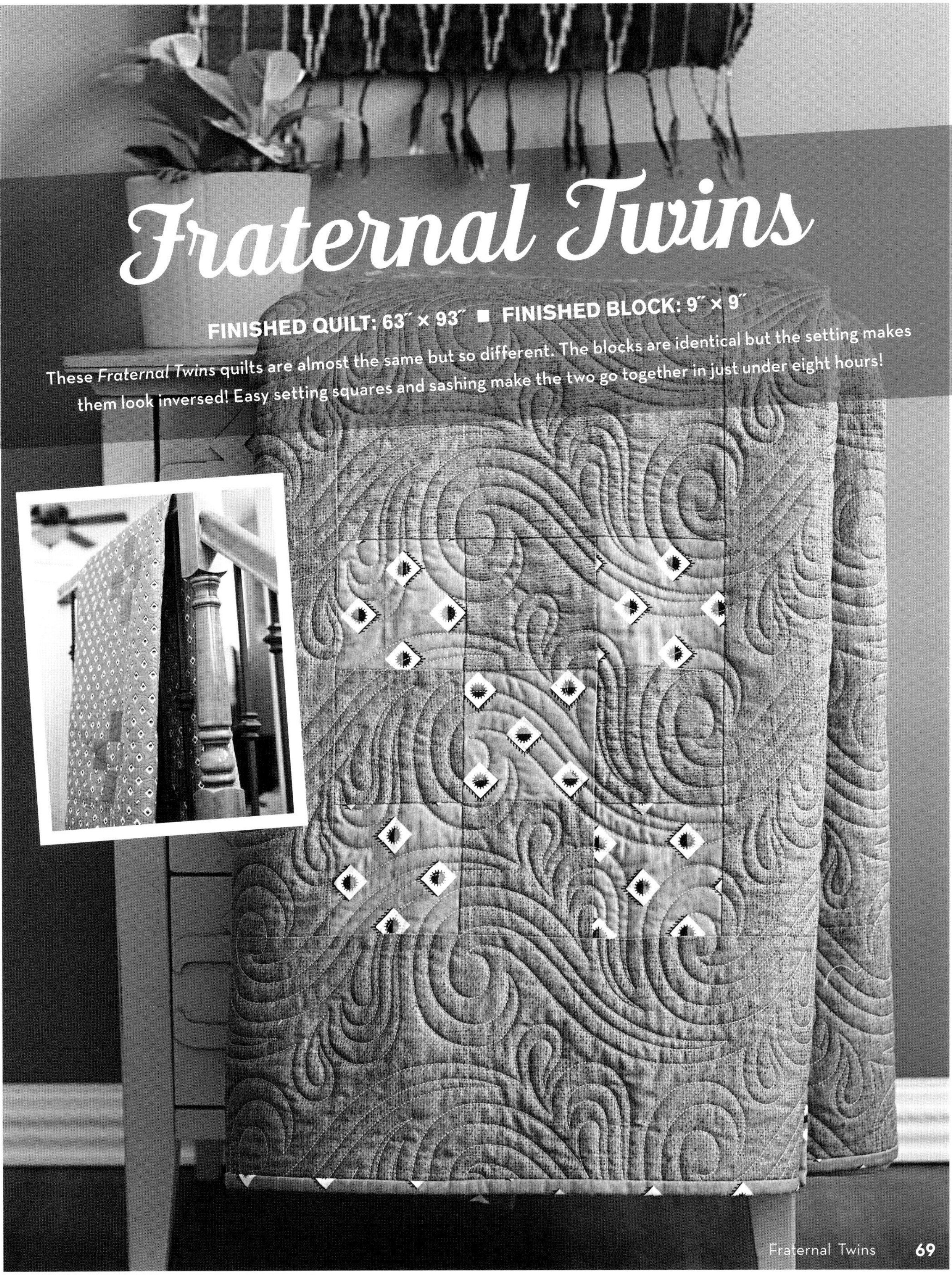

Fabrics

Yardage is based on 42″ usable fabric width. WOF = width of fabric.

Lightweight denim or chambray: 5 yards

Pink polka dot print: 5¼ yards

Backing: 5⅔ yards for each quilt

Batting: 2 pieces 69″ × 99″

Design Notes

These are great quilts to make for your college freshman and roommate! Use their school colors for a personalized touch.

Cutting

DENIM OR CHAMBRAY

Blocks:

Cut 11 strips 3½″ × WOF.

Top and bottom borders:

Cut 3 strips 6½″ × WOF.

Sashing/borders and alternate blocks:

Cut 8 strips 9½″ × WOF for column sashing/borders.

Cut 3 strips 9½″ × WOF; subcut 12 squares 9½″ × 9½″ for alternate blocks.

Binding:

Cut 8 strips 2½″ × WOF.

PINK POLKA DOT

Blocks:

Cut 13 strips 3½″ × WOF.

Top and bottom borders:

Cut 3 strips 6½″ × WOF.

Sashing/borders and alternate blocks:

Cut 8 strips 9½″ × WOF for column sashing/borders.

Cut 3 strips 9½″ × WOF; subcut 12 squares 9½″ × 9½″ for alternate blocks.

Binding:

Cut 8 strips 2½″ × WOF.

Blocks

Use a ¼″ seam allowance. Refer to Strip-Set Construction (page 11) as needed.

> NOTE
>
> Both quilts are made from identical Nine-Patches. The color of the sashing is what makes them look different!

STEP 1 Using 10 pink 3½″ strips and 5 denim 3½″ strips, make 5 strip sets pink / denim / pink.

STEP 2 Using 6 denim 3½″ strips and 3 pink 3½″ strips, make 3 strip sets denim / pink / denim.

STEP 3 Cross-cut all strip sets into 3½″ units. Use 2 units from Step 1 and 1 unit from Step 2 to make a Nine-Patch. Make 30 blocks.

9½″ × 9½″

Assembly

SASHING

STEP 1 Sew 4 pink 9½″ × 9½″ alternate blocks in between 5 Nine-Patches. Make 3 columns.

STEP 2 Sew 2 pink 9½″ × WOF sashing/border strips together end to end. Make 4. Measure the length of each column and cut the 4 sashing/border strips to this length. If the column lengths differ, average the 3 numbers to calculate the correct measurement for cutting.

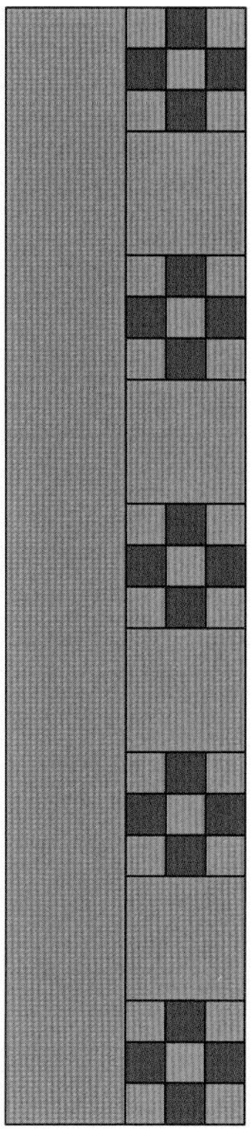

Sashing assembly

STEP 3 Sew a sashing/border strip to the side of each column.

STEP 4 Join the 3 columns and add the remaining sashing/border strip to complete the quilt center (refer to the quilt assembly diagram, page 72).

STEP 5 Repeat Steps 1–4 for the second quilt in the blue colorway.

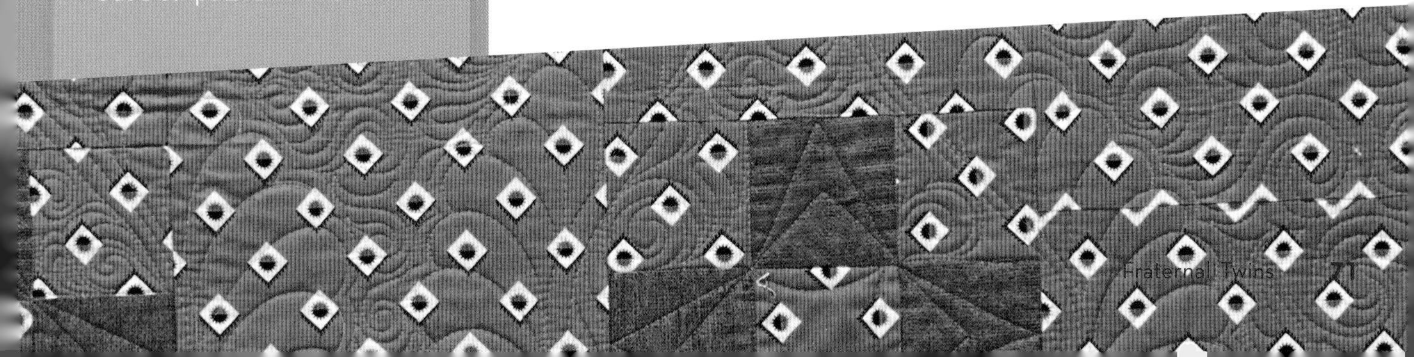

TOP AND BOTTOM BORDERS

STEP 1 Sew the 3 pink 6½″ × WOF strips together end to end. Measure the width of the pink quilt through its center and cut 2 border strips 6½″ × this length.

STEP 2 Sew a border strip to the top and bottom of the pink quilt.

STEP 3 Repeat Steps 1 and 2 for the blue colorway.

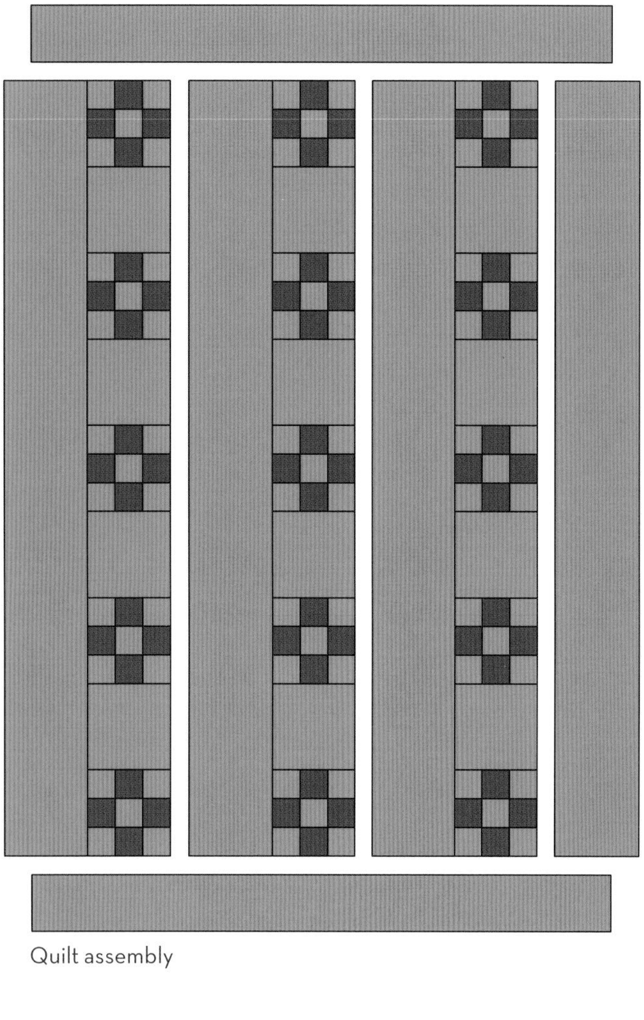

Quilt assembly

Finishing

Refer to Finishing the Quilt (page 12) as needed.

Layer and baste the quilt.

QUILTING

This one is so nice—you will want to make it twice! The simplistic beauty of the quilt can be highlighted with quilting that moves your eye along the quilt.

Quilting a feather in two separate sections is a fun way to use the quilting to play with the "twins" theme of the quilts. Having the feather curve around and between the Nine-Patch blocks ... well, that just takes it to another level of fun!

Fraternal Feathers

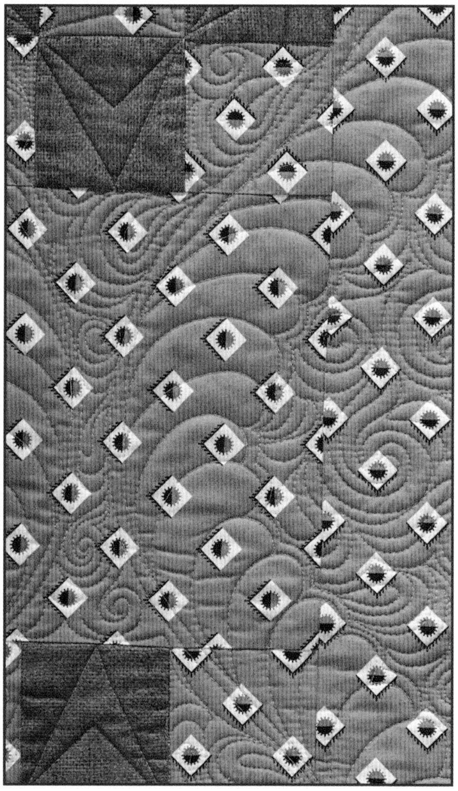

STEP 1 Working along one side of a column of Nine-Patches, quilt a line that curves around the Nine-Patch blocks, almost touching their outermost points. Then, quilt another line that echoes the first line. *Fig. A*

STEP 2 Quilt petals along the line. The petals on this type of feather are quilted in pairs. Quilt a line that curves out and around to touch the petal below it. Travel along the curve until you are on the top of the petal. Curve out and back into the spine of the feather. *Fig. B*

STEP 3 Continue quilting petals until the whole line is filled in with feathers. *Fig. C*

STEP 4 Repeat Steps 1–3, quilting a half-feather on the other side of the Nine-Patch column so that it mirrors the first feather. *Fig. D*

Once you complete the feathers, you can quilt the blocks and fill in any gaps between the feathers with a design such as swirls.

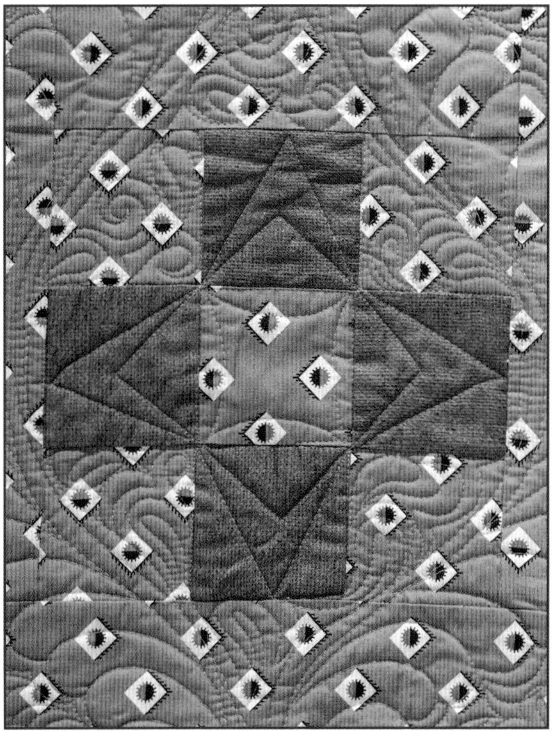

A

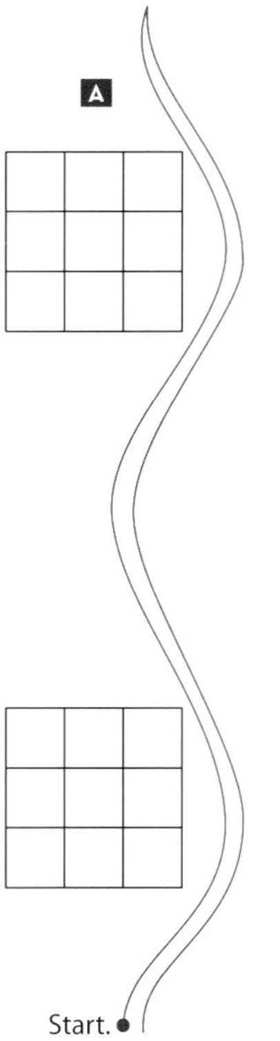

B

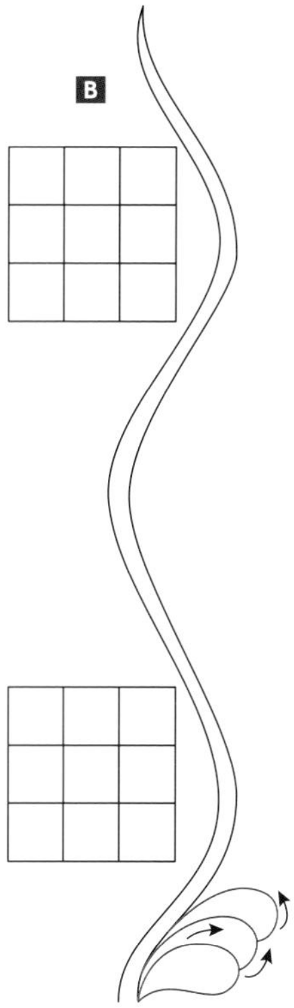

C

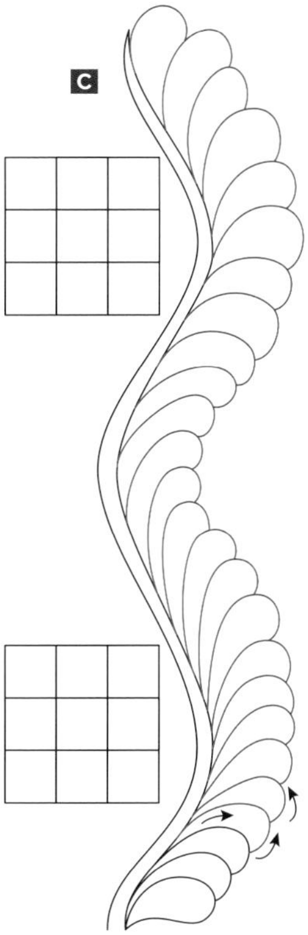

D

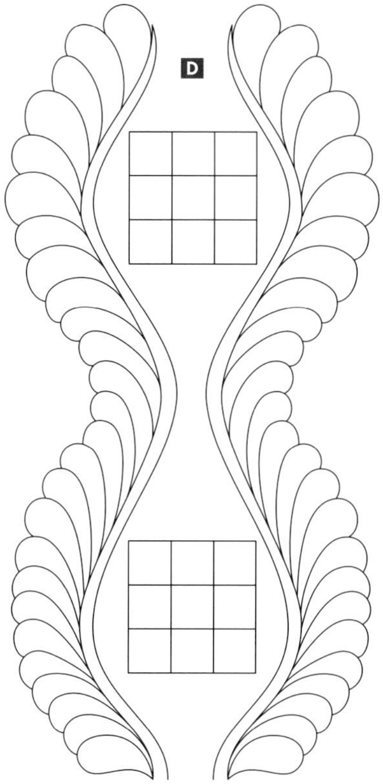

NOTE

If you don't feel like doing so much work, or you need to get the quilt done ASAP, you can quilt an allover design, such as swirls. It's faster and still adds beautiful texture.

Allover design, Harbour Wave pantograph, by Patricia E. Ritter and Marybeth O'Halloran is available at urbanelementz.com (search for Harbour Wave).

THE LAST STEP

Add the binding to your quilt, referring to Binding (page 14) as needed. Note that *Fraternal Twins* requires about 330″ of binding for each quilt.

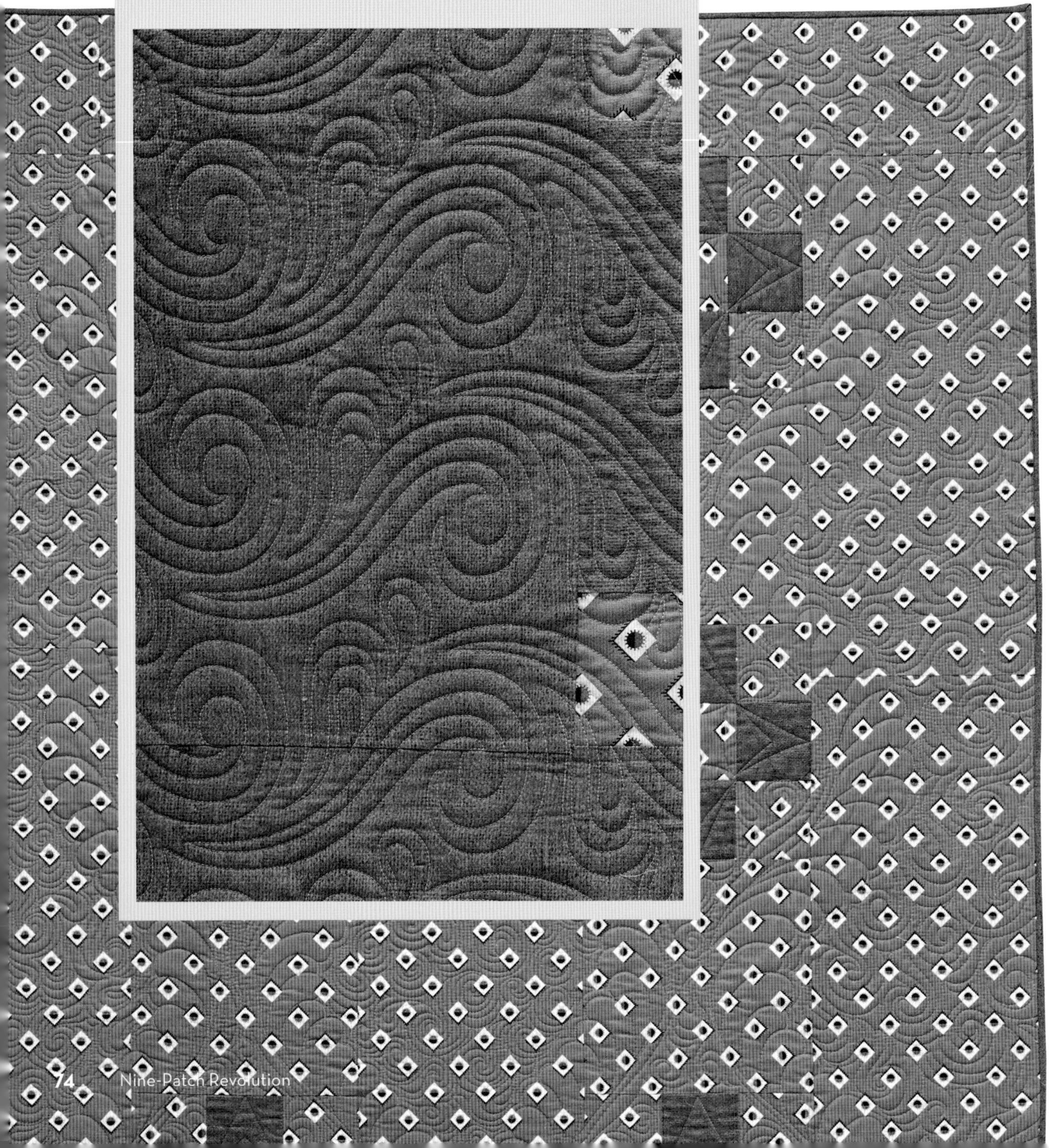

Nine-Patch Chain

FINISHED QUILT: 72″ × 81″ ■ FINISHED BLOCK: 9″ × 9″

Nine-Patch Chain goes together quickly, making it a great choice when you need a quilt in a hurry! Offsetting the color chains with gray and white is the perfect modern accent!

Design Notes

For maximum scrappiness, search your stash for 72 prints in all colors of the rainbow, plus black and gray. If you don't have enough, you can repeat fabrics, making sure to spread them throughout the top so they aren't clumped together.

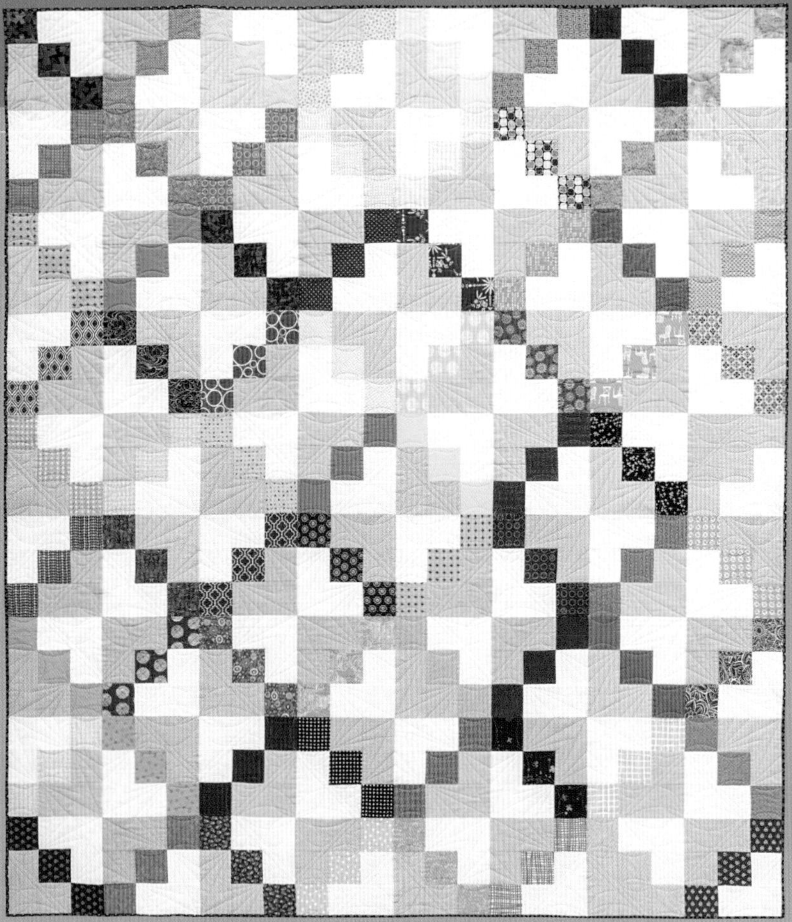

Fabrics

Yardage is based on 42″ usable fabric width. WOF = width of fabric.

Light gray solid: 2½ yards (1⅞ yards for blocks, ⅝ yard for binding)

White solid: 1⅞ yards

Scrap prints: Up to 72 prints, at least 7″ × 7″ square

Coordinating print: 5 yards for backing

Batting: 78″ × 87″

Cutting

LIGHT GRAY

Cut 18 strips 3½″ × WOF; subcut 72 rectangles 6½″ × 3½″ and 72 squares 3½″ × 3½″.

WHITE

Cut 18 strips 3½″ × WOF; subcut 72 rectangles 6½″ × 3½″ and 72 squares 3½″ × 3½″.

SCRAPS

Cut 3 matching print squares 3½″ × 3½″ from each scrap.

BINDING

Cut 8 strips 2½″ × WOF.

Blocks

Use a 1/4″ seam allowance. Refer to Basic Construction (page 8) as needed.

Each block is made with a white square and rectangle, a light gray square and rectangle, and 3 squares of the same print. Lay out the pieces as shown and sew them into rows. Join the rows. Make 63 blocks.

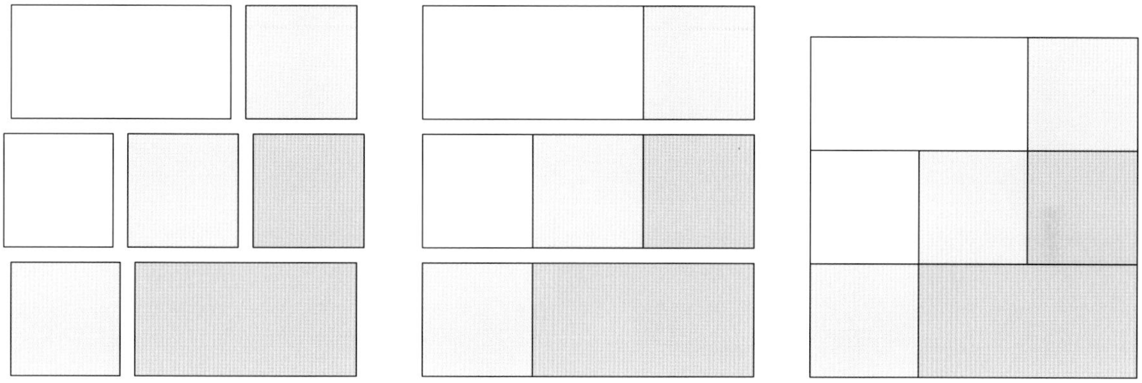

9 1/2″ × 9 1/2″

Assembly

To achieve the chain, sew 9 rows of 8 blocks together, alternating the direction of the print squares on a diagonal from block to block and row to row. Refer to the quilt assembly diagram for placement.

> NOTE
>
> Since each block has a light and dark side, similar to a Log Cabin block, you can set the blocks in many traditional Log Cabin settings. Experiment with different settings on a design wall before sewing together the blocks.

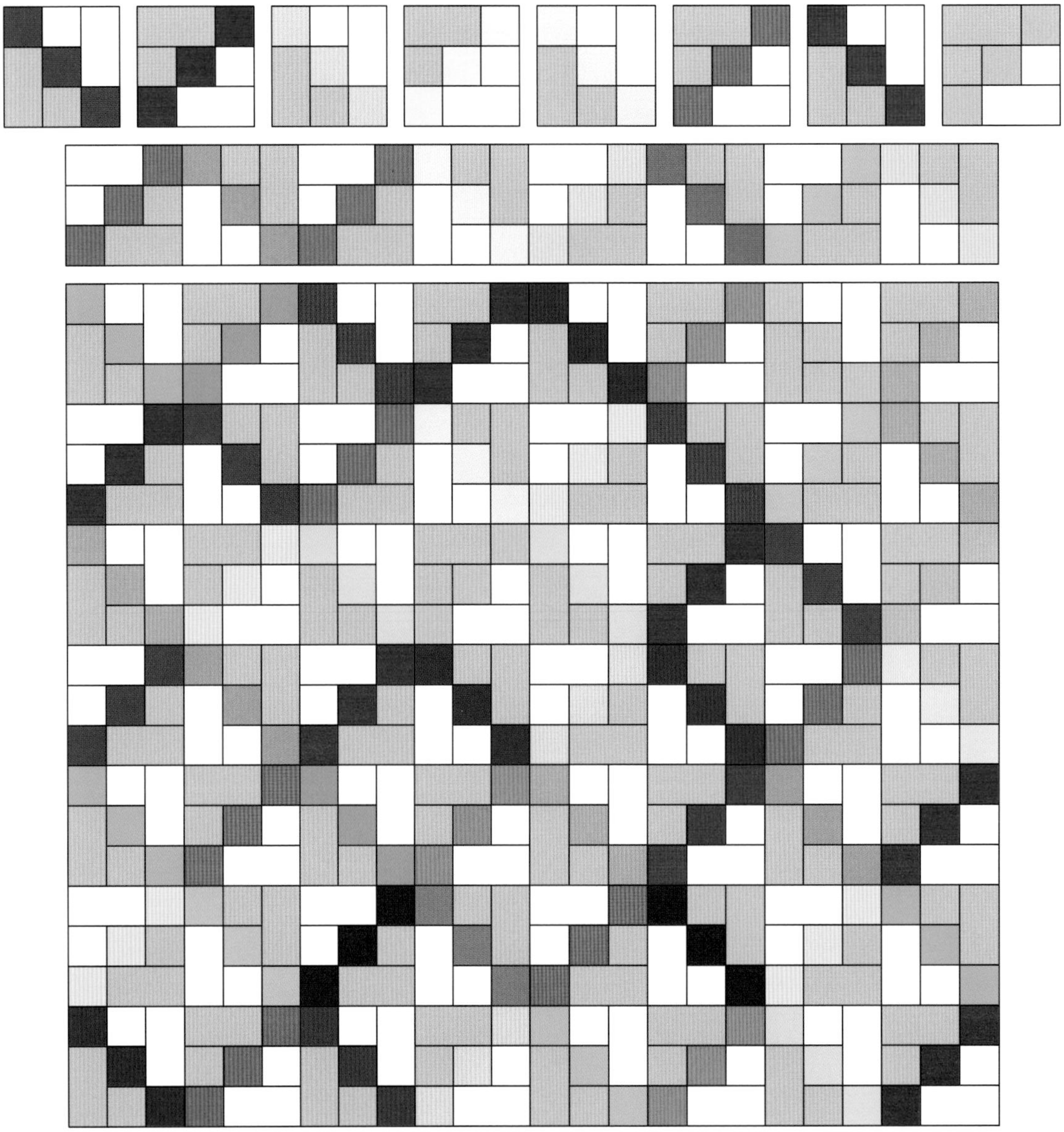

Quilt assembly

Finishing

Refer to Finishing the Quilt (page 12) as needed.

Layer and baste the quilt.

QUILTING

The graphic look of this quilt is just begging for a complex-looking geometric quilt design. But just because it looks complex doesn't mean that it's difficult to quilt. Using reference points on the block as guides for the quilting lines makes it pretty easy once you get the hang of it!

Star Design

STEP 1 Quilt a diagonal line from an outer point to the center and then back to the next outer point. *Fig. A*

STEP 2 Echo inside the line twice more, forming 3 V's. *Fig. B*

STEP 3 Quilt a line above that angles toward the center, stopping about 1″ before. Quilt another line that angles up to the next outer point. *Fig. C*

STEP 4 Repeat Steps 1 and 2 to fill in the top area of the block. *Fig. D*

STEP 5 Continue working around the block, repeating this process and using the outer points as a guide. *Fig. E*

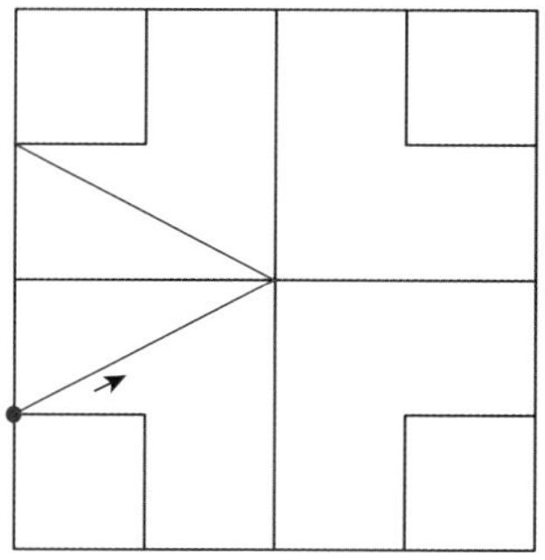

A

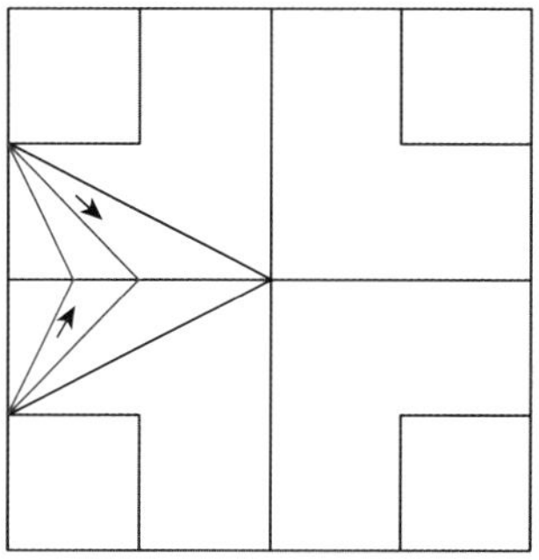

B

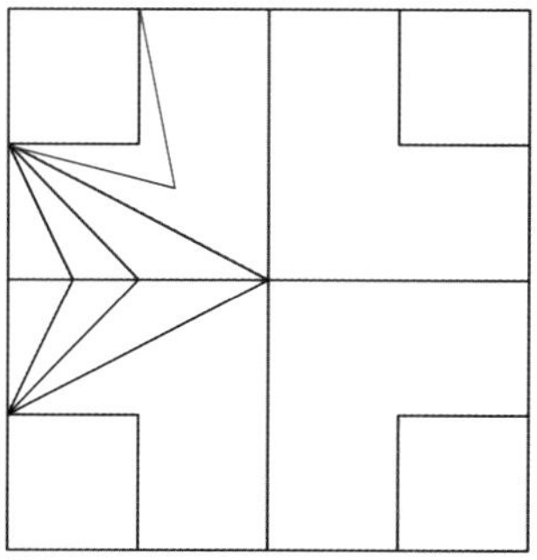

C

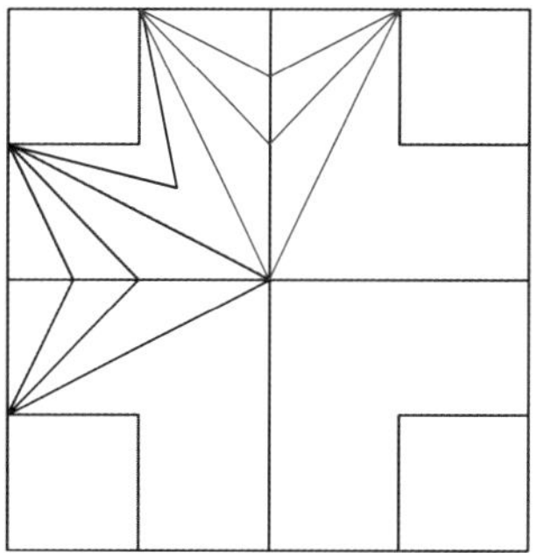

D

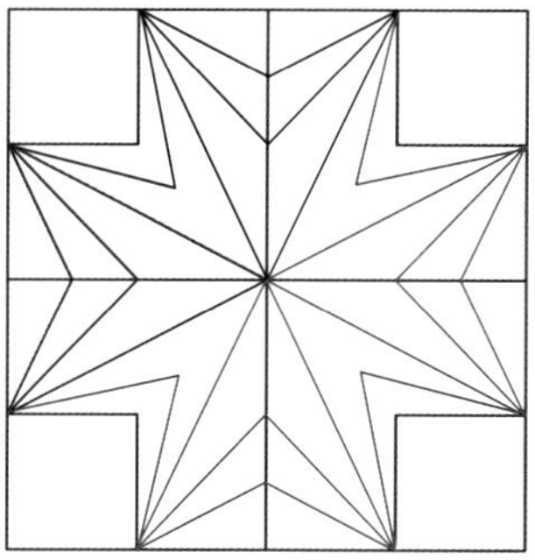

E

THE LAST STEP

Add the binding to your quilt, referring to Binding (page 14) as needed. Note that *Nine-Patch Chain* requires about 320″ of binding.

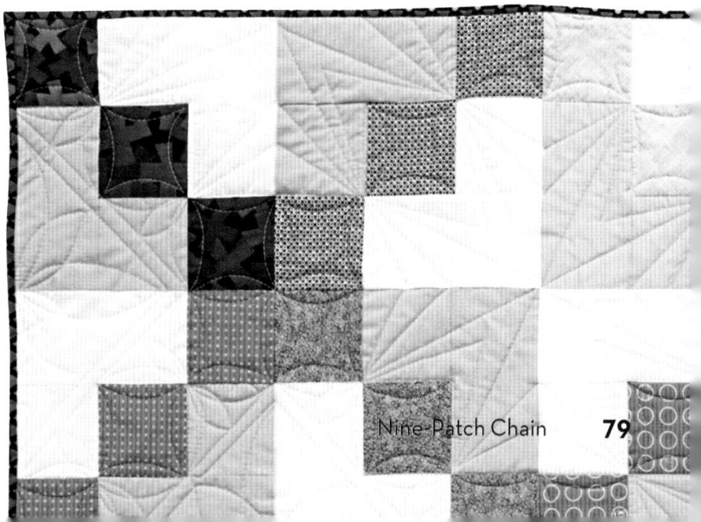

Stretch'd

FINISHED QUILT: 75″ × 90″ ■ FINISHED SMALL BLOCK: 8¼″ × 10½″

FINISHED LARGE BLOCK: 25″ × 30″

The large, expansive blocks make this the perfect minimal quilt for you to experiment with a new quilting design or to improve your skills.

Design Notes

Any three colors will work great with this quilt. Just make sure the values in the small Nine-Patch are close together to keep it a subtle detail.

Fabrics

Yardage is based on 42″ usable fabric width. WOF = width of fabric.

Light blue: 3½ yards

Cream: 3 yards

Medium blue: 1 fat eighth

Binding: ⅝ yard cream or light blue

Backing: 5½ yards

Batting: 81″ × 96″

Cutting

LIGHT BLUE

Cut 4 strips 25½″ × WOF;
subcut 4 rectangles 25½″ × 30½″.

Cut 1 strip 20″ × WOF;
subcut 1 rectangle 25½″ × 20″,
1 rectangle 11″ × 17¼″, and
4 rectangles 3¼″ × 4″.

CREAM

Cut 4 strips 25½″ × WOF;
subcut 4 rectangles 25½″ × 30½″.

MEDIUM BLUE

Cut 5 rectangles 3¼″ × 4″.

BINDING

Cut 9 strips 2½″ × WOF.

Blocks

Use a ¼″ seam allowance. Refer to Basic Construction (page 8) as needed.

NINE-PATCH BLOCKS

Using the 5 medium blue 3¼″ × 4″ rectangles and the 4 light blue 3¼″ × 4″ rectangles, make 1 Nine-Patch block.

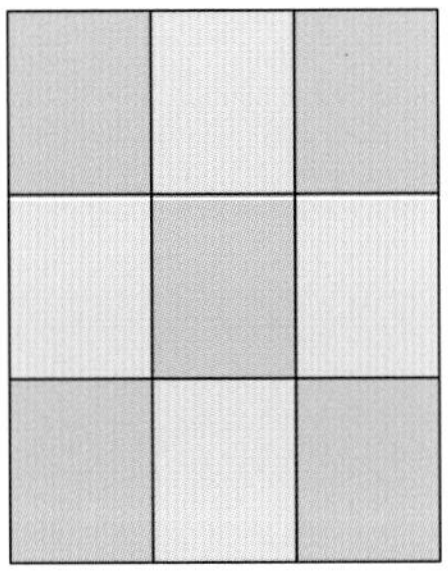

8¾″ × 11

CENTER RECTANGLE

Sew the Nine-Patch to the rectangle along the 11″ side. Press toward the rectangle. Lay the Nine-Patch / rectangle unit right side up, Nine-Patch to the left. Sew the 25½″ × 20″ rectangle to the top matching the 25½″ sides. The Nine-Patch should be on the bottom left of the block.

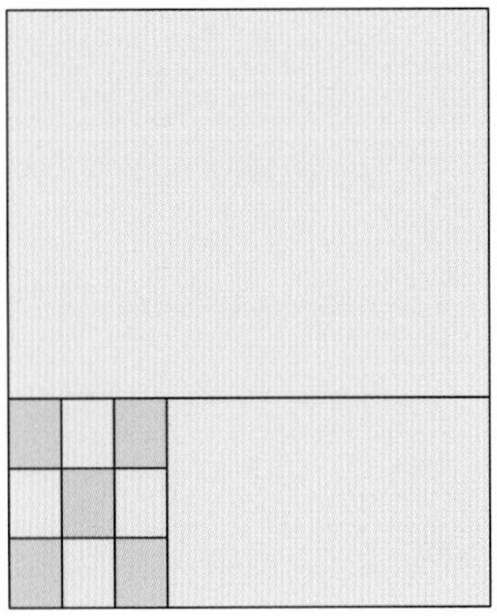

25½″ × 30½″

Assembly

Lay out the rectangles in 3 rows of 3, alternating the blue and cream. Sew them together in rows, and then join the rows.

Quilt assembly

Finishing

Refer to Finishing the Quilt (page 12) as needed.

Layer and baste the quilt.

QUILTING

This huge Nine-Patch quilt with the baby version in the center is quick to put together, meaning you can get to the quilting even faster. Could anything be more fun than that? Let the big blocks be your guide, and try alternating designs in the blue and white fabrics.

The offset squares design is perfect for the larger areas in this quilt. It adds a nice consistency, while not overpowering the smaller block in the center. It's quick to quilt and even has a fun secondary design within itself.

Alternating between echoed squares and the box with free-motion quilting results in a fun secondary design where the blocks create almost a diagonal line. If you want, however, you can quilt just one option for a nice allover design.

Offset Squares

While there are a lot of straight lines in this design, a walking foot or a ruler isn't really necessary. All the straight lines are fairly short, meaning that you can freehand them and keep them somewhat straight.

STEP 1 Starting about ½″ down from the upper corner, quilt a square spiral that echoes in on itself. Once you reach the center, quilt a line that extends to the right past the block. Try to make the line a little bit wider than the square itself. *Fig. A*

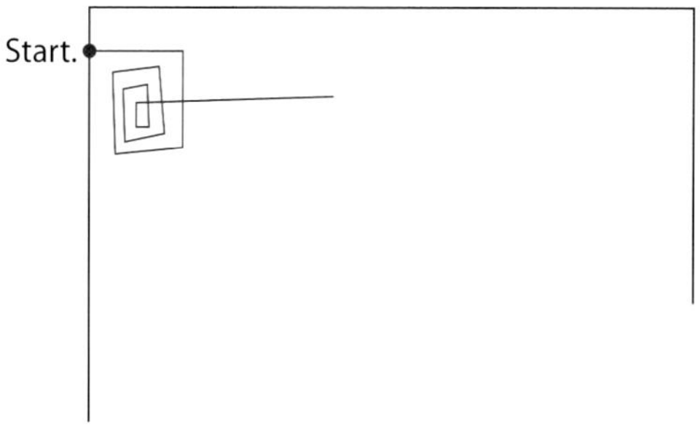

A

NOTE

Your squares can be as big or as little as you like, just try to keep them all the same size to help make the rows as even as possible.

STEP 2 Quilt a closed square by quilting a line up, to the right, down, to the left and back up to the starting point. *Fig. B*

STEP 3 Fill in the closed square with a free-motion quilting design, such as a meander or swirl, working your way across to the other side of the box. *Fig. C*

STEP 4 Quilt a line that extends from the box (make it a little longer than the width of the boxes) and quilt another echoed square. Repeat this process, quilting echoed squares, closed boxes, and spaces, until you reach the end of the area. *Fig. D*

> **NOTE**
>
> You don't have to end on a space, or even a particular square. Just go until you run out of room, even if it means that the last thing in the row is wider or narrower than the rest.

STEP 5 Travel up the side of the area ½″ above the quilting. Fill in the space above the row by echoing the boxes and spaces until the area is filled in. Try to end on the right side of the area. *Fig. E*

STEP 6 Quilt a line that echoes the first row about ½″ away back to the left side of the area. *Fig. F*

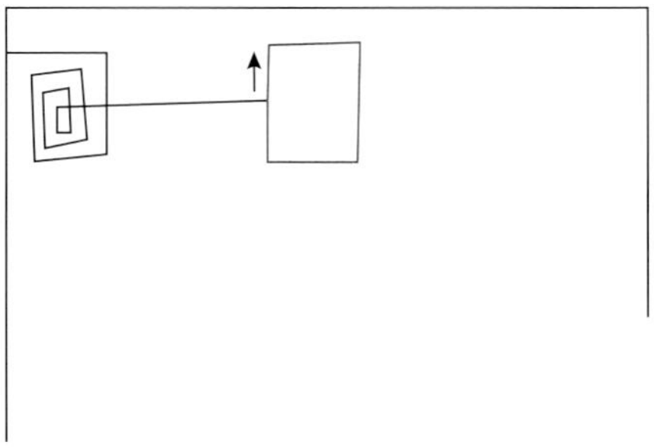

B

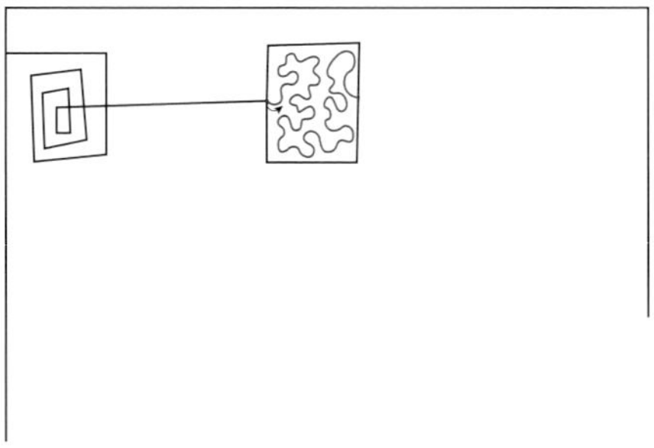

C

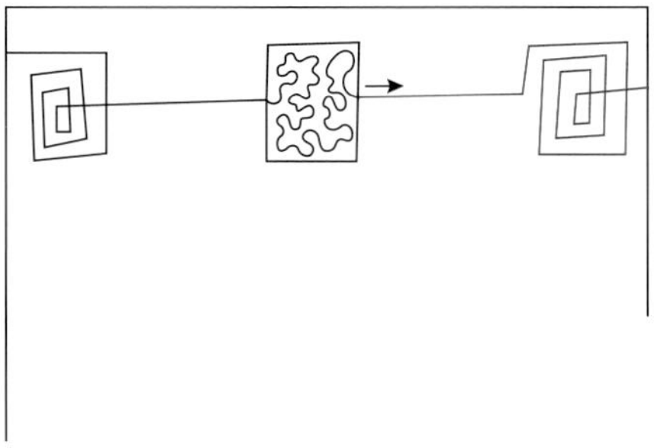

D

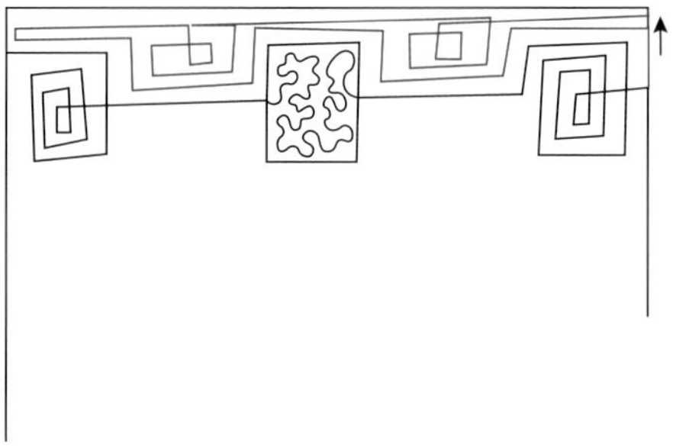

E

F

STEP 7 For the second row, quilt the same shapes, except where there is a box in the row above, quilt a space. Where there is a space, quilt a box or echoed square. Continue until you reach the right side of the area. *Fig. G*

STEP 8 Travel down the edge about ½″ and echo the row quilted in Step 7 back to the left side. *Fig. H*

STEP 9 Continue quilting rows and echoing until the area is filled in. *Fig. I*

G

H

I

Small Nine-Patch

Even though the offset squares design doesn't detract from other piecing, you might want to echo around the small Nine-Patch block a few times to help separate it from the rest of the quilting. This helps prevent it from getting swallowed up by the larger quilting areas.

THE LAST STEP

Add the binding to your quilt, referring to Binding (page 14) as needed. Note that *Stretch'd* requires about 345″ of binding.

Plaid

FINISHED QUILT: 60″ × 72″ ■ FINISHED BLOCK: 12″ × 12″

Plaid in bright colors is a cheerful optical illusion! The continuous gray forces the color to recede to the background, creating an illusion of gray crosses hovering over the bright colors.

Design Notes

This quilt also looks stunning in black, medium gray, and light gray for a more masculine look.

Fabrics

Yardage is based on 42″ usable fabric width. WOF = width of fabric.

Assorted solids: Fat eighths of 30 different solids

Medium gray: 1 yard

Binding: ⅝ yard medium gray

Backing: 4 yards gray solid

Batting: 66″ × 78″

Cutting

ASSORTED SOLIDS

From each solid:

Cut 1 square 6½″ × 6½″.

Cut 2 rectangles 2½″ × 6½″.

Cut 1 square 4½″ × 4½″.

Cut 1 square 2½″ × 2½″.

MEDIUM GRAY

Cut 6 strips 4½″ × WOF; subcut 24 rectangles 4½″ × 6½″ and 24 rectangles 4½″ × 2½″.

BINDING

Cut 7 strips 2½″ × WOF.

Blocks

Use a ¼″ seam allowance. Refer to Basic Construction (page 8) as needed.

Each block is made of the following:

Solid color:

- 1 square 6½″ × 6½″
- 2 rectangles 2½″ × 6½″
- 1 square 4½″ × 4½″
- 1 square 2½″ × 2½″

Medium gray:

- 2 rectangles 4½″ × 6½″
- 2 rectangles 4½″ × 2½″

Lay out the 5 matching solid color and 4 medium gray pieces as shown. Sew them together. Press the seams open. Make 30 blocks.

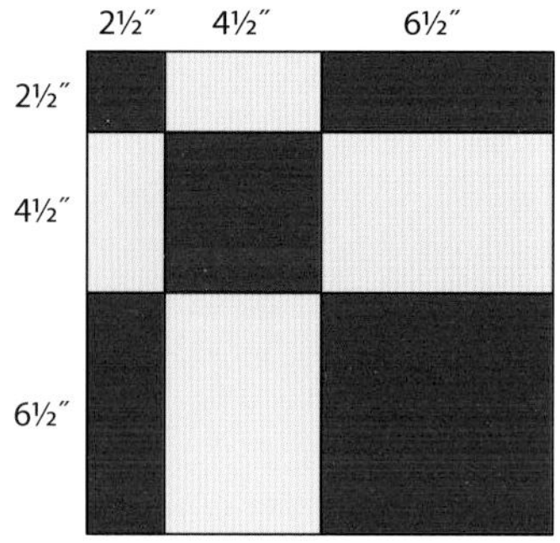

12½″ × 12½″

Assembly

Lay out the blocks in 6 rows of 5 blocks each. Make sure the color distribution is pleasing to your eye. Sew them together in rows, and then join the rows.

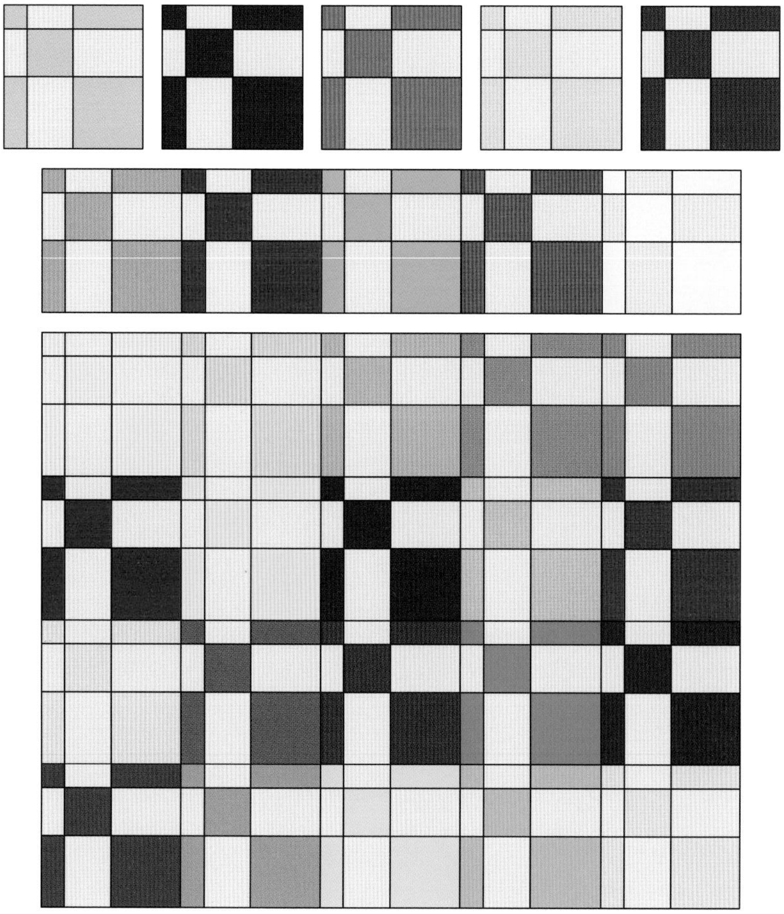

Quilt assembly

Finishing

Refer to Finishing the Quilt (page 12) as needed.

Layer and baste the quilt.

QUILTING

The differently sized patches in this quilt add a look of randomness, but that doesn't mean that the quilting needs to be random. Instead of focusing on the whole block, you can quilt a different design in each portion of the block, regardless of the fabric color. You just might have a blast coming up with so many different designs!

Continuous curves (page 13) are perfect for small patches, and concentric squares echo the sides of the rectangular patches. You can also throw in a few swirls for fun!

But why should the colored patches have all the quilting fun? Try combining overlapping ribbon candy with echo lines in the gray—it gives the quilt the illusion of being woven together.

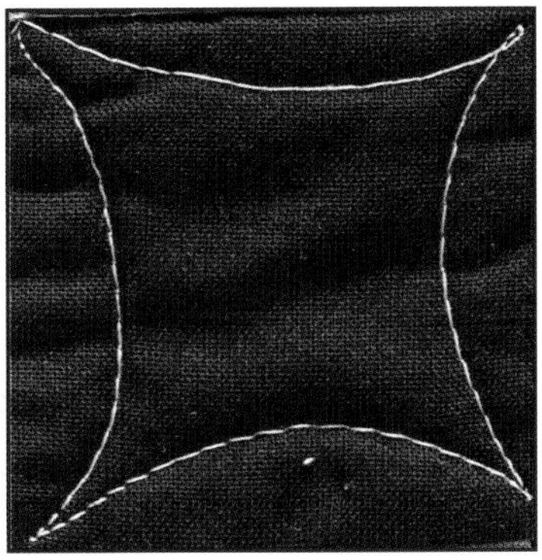

Continuous curves in small squares

Swirls are great fillers for larger blocks.

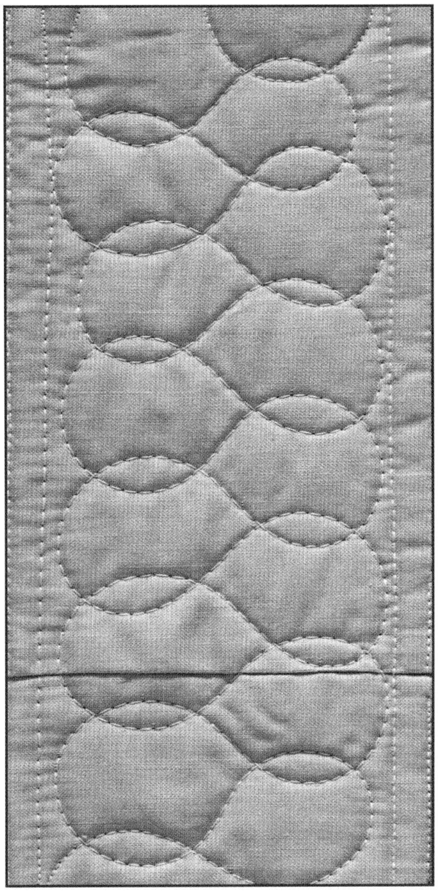

Concentric squares in skinny blocks

Ribbon Candy Echoes

STEP 1 Quilt a line ¼″ inside a long side of the block. Stop at the edge and quilt along the seam until you are ¼″ away from the opposite side. *Fig. A*

STEP 2 Quilt another echo line ¼″ away from the opposite side of the block, stopping at the edge. *Fig. B*

STEP 3 From the side of the block, quilt a line that curves out and back. It should look almost like an S. *Fig. C*

STEP 4 Continue curving away from the bottom and then back toward it, overlapping the first S-shape by about ¼″. *Fig. D*

STEP 5 Continue to repeat the shape, filling in the space between the echo lines. Work your way to the other side of the block. *Fig. E*

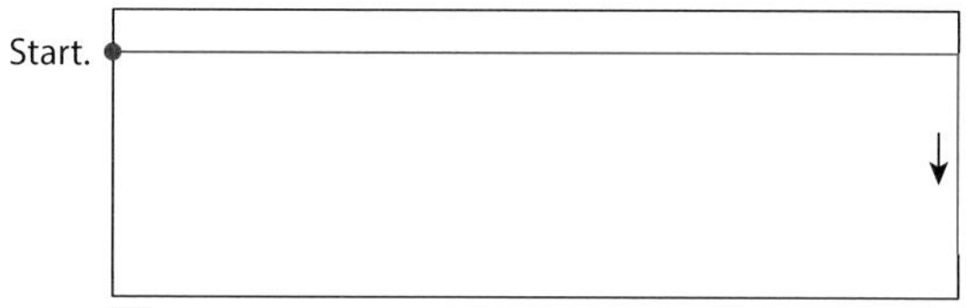

A

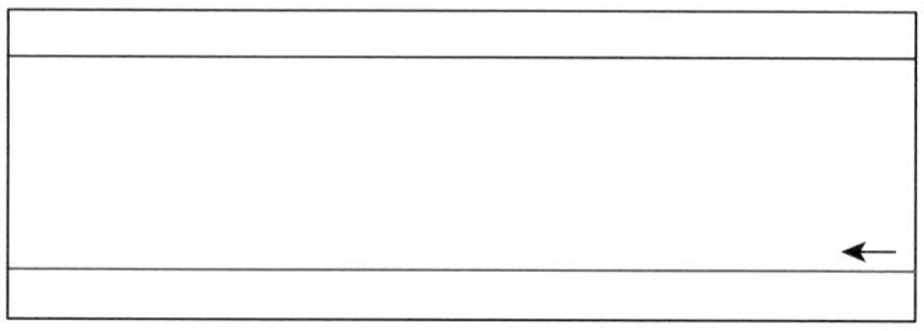

B

C

D

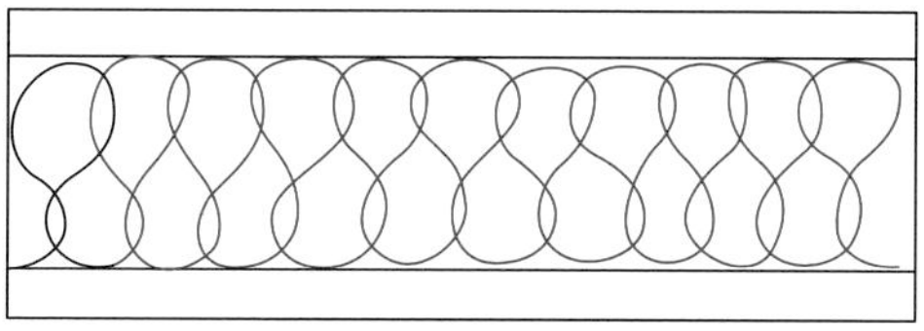

E

Tip

If you're having trouble quilting this design, try tracing over the diagram (Figs. C–E). It will help you learn how the design flows.

Of course, you don't have to match these exact quilting designs. Try experimenting with some of your favorites and see what you can come up with!

THE LAST STEP

Add the binding to your quilt, referring to Binding (page 14) as needed. Note that *Plaid* requires about 280″ of binding.

Camo

FINISHED QUILT: 90″ × 90″ ■ FINISHED BLOCK: 18″ × 18″

Camo is a scrap-busting controlled improv quilt made of nine panels in nine different color families. Each panel is a mix of print and solids in values from the lightest lights to the darkest darks. The wide borders give you plenty of room to have fun quilting!

Design Notes

This quilt is made specifically for a platform bed—one with no footboard. By adding the pieced strip along the bottom edge, the quilt has a little extra interest when viewed on a bed.

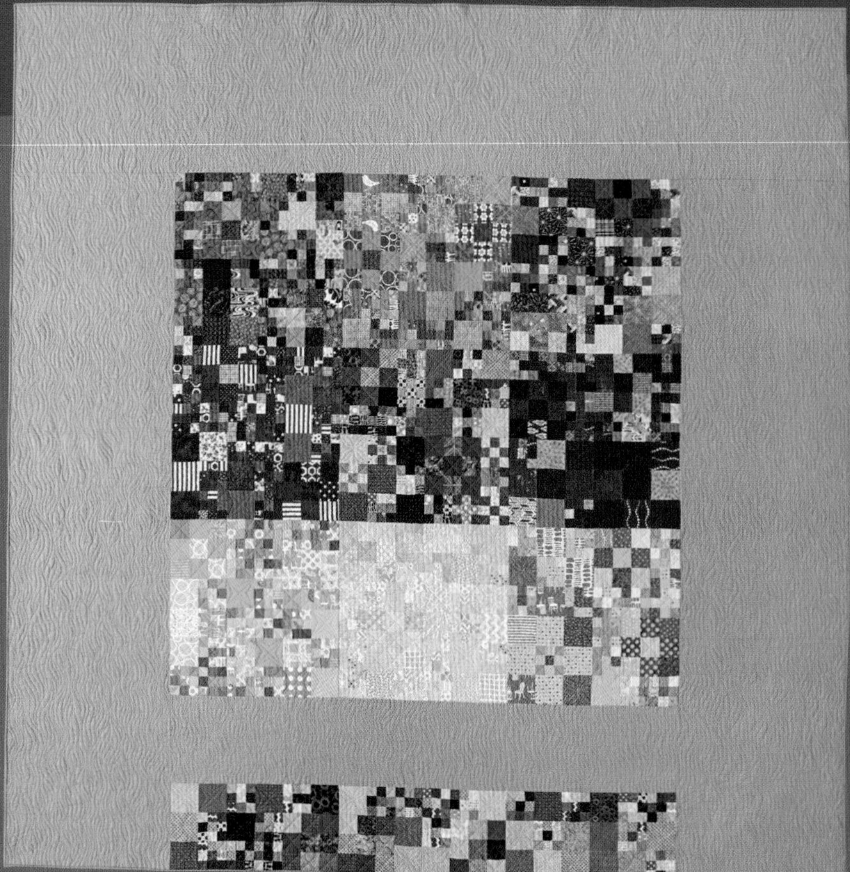

Fabrics

Yardage is based on 42″ usable fabric width. WOF = width of fabric.

Scraps in small prints and solids: A good collection in 9 colors (such as red, pink, orange, yellow, green, blue, aqua, purple, and black/gray).

Note: Be sure to include a wide range of values from light to dark in the widest variety of fabrics possible. The more scraps, the better. Since this is mostly improv-pieced, the amount of each fabric will be determined by how much variety you want and how many scraps you have on hand.

Medium gray: 4½ yards for borders and binding

Batting: 96″ × 96″

Backing: 8¼ yards

Cutting

MEDIUM GRAY

Borders:

Cut 6 strips 18½″ × WOF.

Cut 2 strips 9½″ × WOF.

Binding:

Cut 9 strips 2½″ × WOF.

Blocks

Use a 1/4″ seam allowance. Refer to Basic Construction (page 8) as needed.

LARGE BLOCKS

Make 9 blocks 18½″ × 18½″ *unfinished* in 9 color families.

Each block is made of various-size Nine-Patch units that, when joined together, creates a pixilated illusion. The more variety of fabrics used, the more pixilated the quilt will look. To make the quilt more visually interesting, make sure to make some Nine-Patch units with only 2 colors to grab the eye off the pixilated background. Make sure the 2 fabrics are close in value so it's subtle and not too jarring.

Each 18″ × 18″ finished block is comprised of finished 3″, 6″, and 9″ blocks that fit together. Oftentimes I used 3″ Nine-Patches together with 3½″ squares to make a 9″ block.

NOTE

Make only a few 9″ × 9″ units per color family and fill in with 6″ × 6″ and 3″ × 3″ to make each block. You want more of the smaller units than the larger ones to keep the pixilating theme.

From each color family, cut squares 1½″ × 1½″, 2½″ × 2½″, and 3½″ × 3½″. Use 9 squares of each size to piece the Nine-Patches. Make some totally random, with up to 9 different fabrics, and make some like a true Nine-Patch, with only 2 colors. Press the seams open. Make 9.

18½″ × 18½″

SMALL BLOCKS

Make 6 blocks $9\frac{1}{2}'' \times 9\frac{1}{2}''$ *unfinished* in gray.

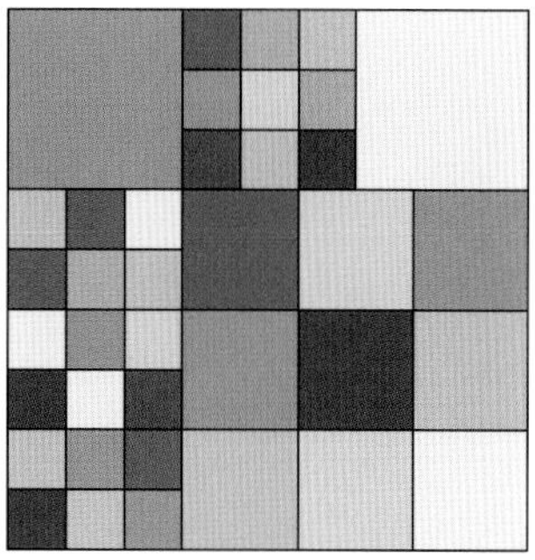

9½″ × 9½″

From the gray prints, cut squares 1½″ × 1½″, 2½″ × 2½″, and 3½″ × 3½″, with fewer 3½″ × 3½″.

Make 6 blocks that finish 9″ × 9″ in the same manner you made the large blocks.

Assembly

BLOCKS

STEP 1 Lay out the 9 large blocks as desired. You can place them in rainbow order or, as I did, with the warm colors in the center and the cool colors on the corners with black in the middle.

STEP 2 Sew the blocks into 3 rows of 3 blocks each. Press.

STEP 3 For the bottom pieced strip in shades of gray, lay out the 6 blocks as desired and sew them together. Press.

BORDERS

STEP 1 Sew the 9½″ × WOF strips together in a continuous strip. Repeat with the 18½″ × WOF strips.

STEP 2 Measure the quilt top center through the middle both from side to side and from top to bottom. It should be about 54½″ × 54½″.

STEP 3 Cut the 9½″ strip to the measurement taken in Step 2. Sew to the bottom. Press toward the gray.

STEP 4 Sew the gray pieced strip to the bottom of this unit. Press. Measure through the middle of the quilt from top to bottom. This should be about 72½″.

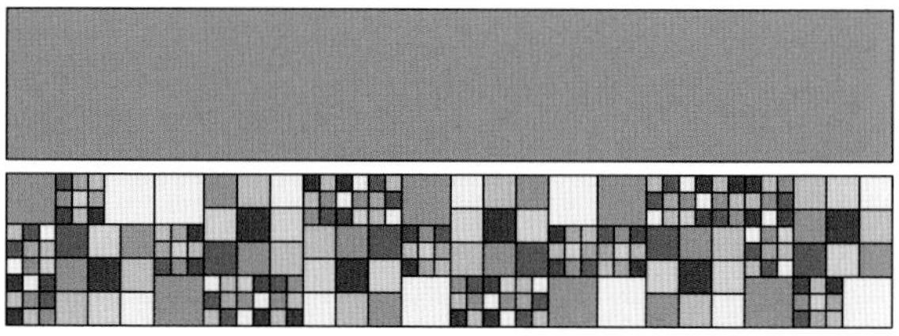

Bottom border assembly

STEP 5 Cut 2 borders the length of the quilt from the 18½″ × WOF strip. Sew to each side, and press.

STEP 6 Measure the quilt through the middle from side to side and cut the remaining border that length. It should be about 90½″. Sew to the top and press.

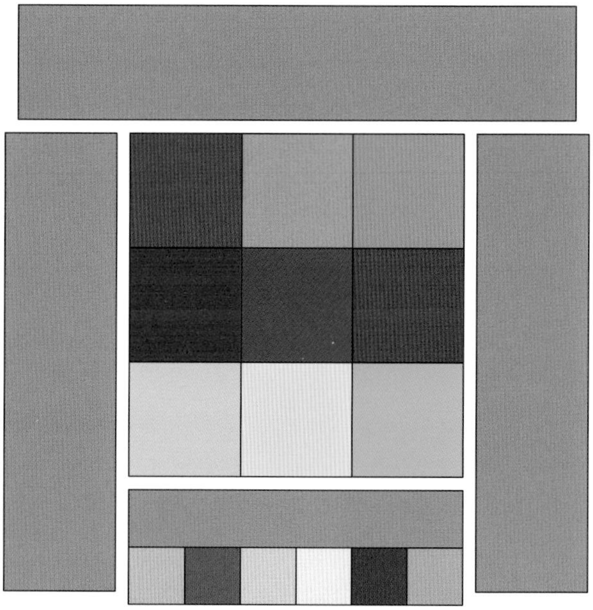

Quilt assembly

Finishing

Refer to Finishing the Quilt (page 12) as needed.

Layer and baste the quilt.

QUILTING

To say that the piecing and colors used in this quilt are stunning is an understatement. Combined with the large gray border, it's just too much fun to quilt! With so many different options, it can be overwhelming deciding which quilting designs to use.

Background

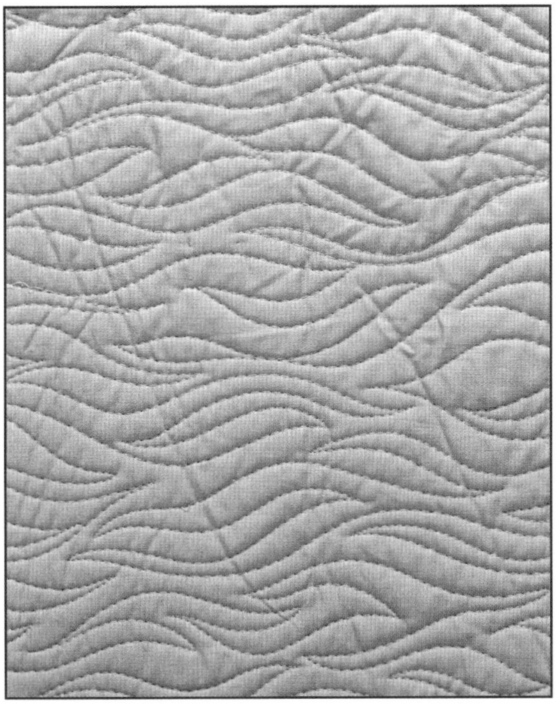

Quilting anything too complex in such a large area can detract from the beautiful piecing in the center. A wavy line design is quick to quilt and has a lovely texture. Any other allover design will produce a wonderful result.

In the Blocks

Since there are three types of blocks that make up the larger patchwork sections, try picking a simple design for each shape. They could even be variations of the same design, such as an X. Doing this gives the quilting a cohesive look, while still highlighting the differences between the blocks.

SMALL NINE-PATCH BLOCKS

Combine straight lines and curves to quickly quilt the Nine-Patch blocks. If quilted in the correct order, this design stops on the opposite side of the block from the starting point so you can go right into quilting the next block. This makes it an efficient way to work your way through the quilt.

STEP 1 Quilt a diagonal line from a corner to the opposite corner. Travel along the edge and quilt another diagonal line toward the opposite corner, stopping at the inside corner of the outer square. *Fig. A*

STEP 2 Quilt continuous curves (page 13) in the 4 center squares of the Nine-Patch. *Fig. B*

STEP 3 Continue quilting the diagonal line until you reach the corner. *Fig. C*

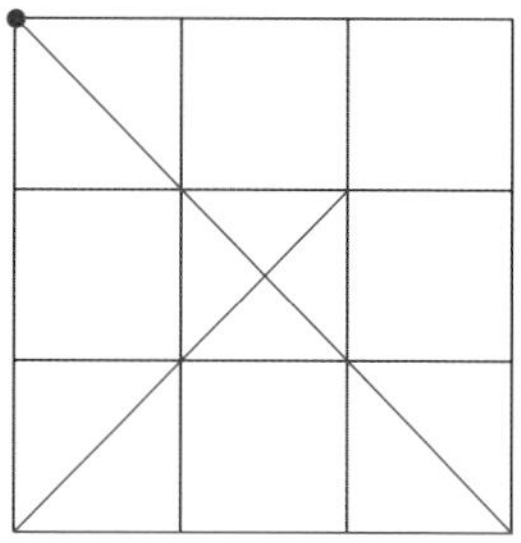

A

B

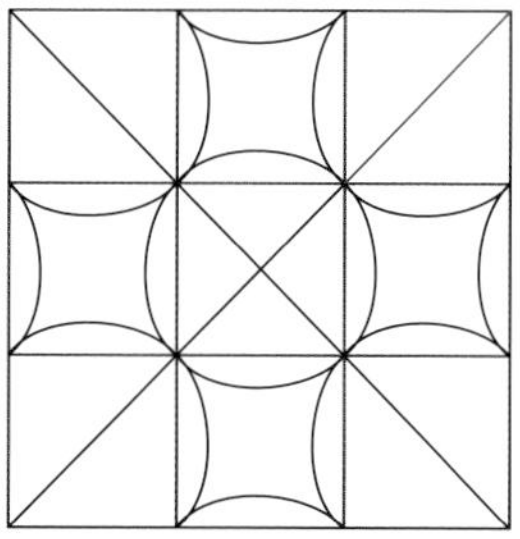

C

THE LAST STEP

Add the binding to your quilt, referring to Binding (page 14) as needed. Note that *Camo* requires about 375″ of binding.

Poppy: A Modern Reproduction

FINISHED QUILT: 90″ × 90″ ■ FINISHED BLOCK: 22½″ × 22½″

It's often said that the best way to honor an antique quilt is to reproduce it. This quilt is a reproduction of a well-loved nineteenth-century quilt. The maker obviously used different blacks that faded to two different grays. She also placed the right side toward the sun for too long, fading the red to a wonderful hot pink. The three greens were probably included when she ran out of red and had three more blocks to finish!

The surprise is that there is no original antique quilt—this is a reproduction of a quilt that never was!

Design Notes

Since these poppies are basically fantasy flowers, you can choose to make them any color you like!

Fabrics

Yardage is based on 42″ usable fabric width. WOF = width of fabric.

Red: 3⅝ yards

Dark gray: 2⅝ yards (2 yards for blocks, ⅝ yard for binding)

Medium gray: 1⅛ yards

Greens (3): ½ yard each of 3 gradations

Hot pink: ½ yard

Backing: 8¼ yards (I used dark gray.)

Batting: 96″ × 96″

Cutting

RED

Cut 5 strips 8⅜″ × WOF; subcut 23 squares 8⅜″ × 8⅜″.

Cut 10 strips 8″ × WOF; subcut 49 squares 8″ × 8″.

HOT PINK

Cut 3 squares 8⅜″ × 8⅜″.

Cut 3 squares 8″ × 8″.

DARK GRAY

Half-square triangle units:

Cut 5 strips 8⅜″ × WOF; subcut 23 squares 8⅜″ × 8⅜″.

Nine-Patch units:

Cut 6 strips 3″ × WOF.

Binding:

Cut 9 strips 2½″ × WOF.

MEDIUM GRAY

Half-square triangle units:

Cut 2 strips 8⅜″ × WOF; subcut 10 squares 8⅜″ × 8⅜″.

Nine-Patch units:

Cut 5 strips 3″ × WOF.

GRADATED GREENS

From each green:

Cut 4 squares 8″ × 8″.

Cut 2 squares 8⅜″ × 8⅜″.

Blocks

Use a ¼″ seam allowance. Refer to Strip-Set Construction (page 11) as needed.

NINE-PATCH UNITS

STEP 1 Using 4 dark gray 3″ × WOF strips and 2 medium gray 3″ × WOF strips, make 2 dark / medium / dark gray strip sets.

STEP 2 Using 2 medium gray 3″ × WOF strips and 1 dark gray 3″ × WOF strip, make 1 medium / dark / medium gray strip set.

STEP 3 Cut the strip sets into 3″ units. You will need a total of 28 units from the Step 1 strip sets; 14 of the Step 2 strip set. Piece the units together to make 14 Nine-Patches.

STEP 4 Subcut the remaining dark gray strip into 10 squares 3″ × 3″ and the remaining light gray strip into 8 squares 3″ × 3″. Make 2 more Nine-Patches with these squares for a total of 16 Nine-Patches.

8″ × 8″

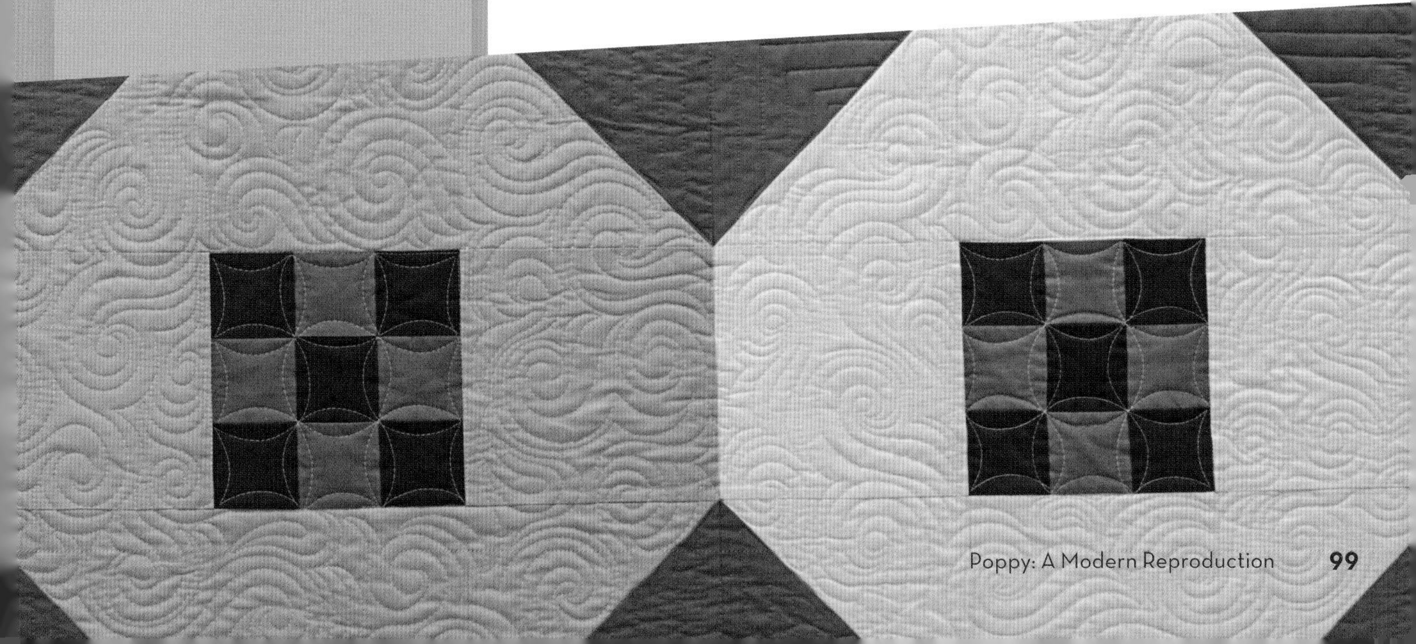

Half-Square Triangle Units Chart

Use the following chart to match 8³/₈″ × 8³/₈″ squares to make the half-square triangles.

Block number	Half-square triangle color pairs	Number of 8³/₈″ × 8³/₈″ squares in each color	Number of blocks required (64 total)
1, 3, 5	Dark gray / Red	18	35
3, 4, 5	Dark gray / Hot pink	3	6
6	Dark gray / Dark green	2	4
2, 4	Med. gray / Red	6	11
7	Med. gray / Med. green	2	4
8	Med. gray / Light green	2	4

Match 2 squares 8³/₈″ × 8³/₈″, right sides together. Draw a line corner to corner on the back of the lightest square. Sew ¼″ from the drawn line on each side. Cut apart on the drawn line. Press the seams *open*.

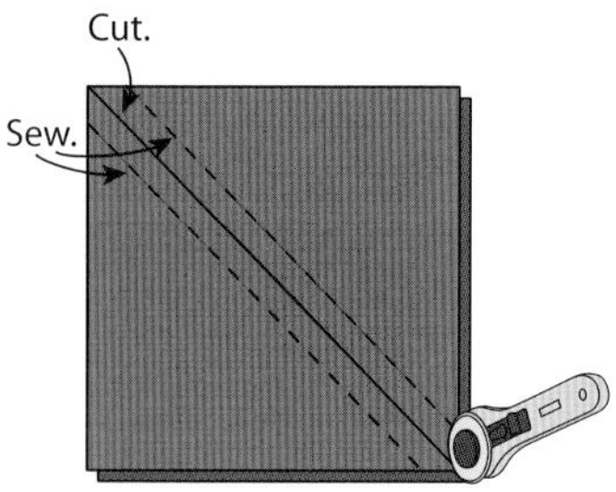

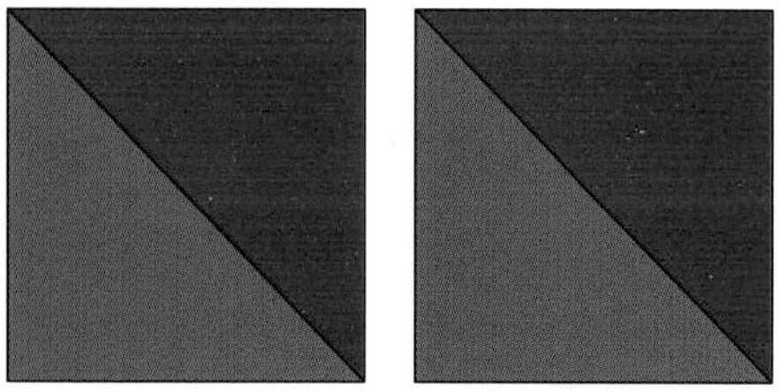
8″ × 8″

BLOCK ASSEMBLY

STEP 1 Lay out 4 half-square triangle units, 4 squares 8″ × 8″, and 1 Nine-Patch per block as shown.

STEP 2 Sew them together by row, pressing the top and bottom row seams toward the center square and pressing the middle row seams away from the Nine-Patch.

STEP 3 Join the rows.

There are 8 configurations of blocks. Make the number of each block specified below.

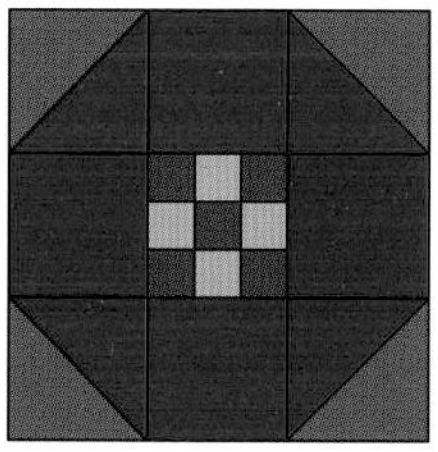
Block 1: Make 7.

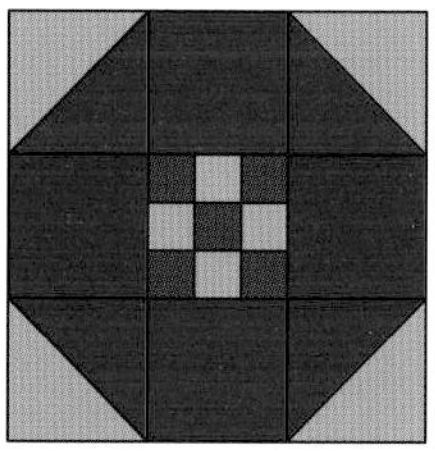
Block 2: Make 2.

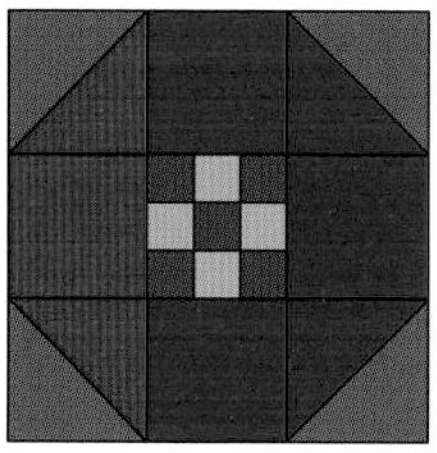
Block 3: Make 2.

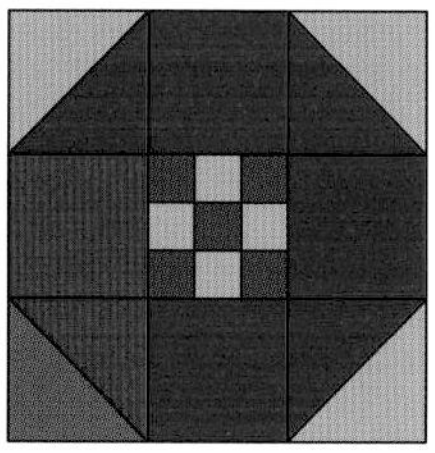
Block 4: Make 1.

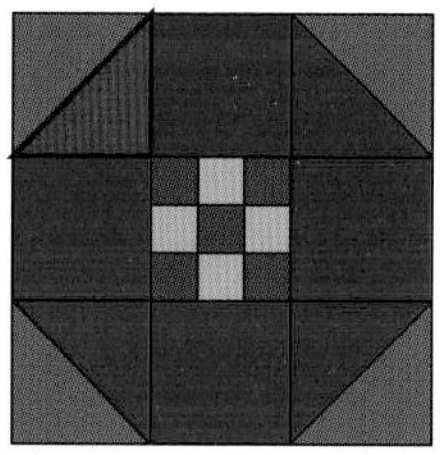
Block 5: Make 1.

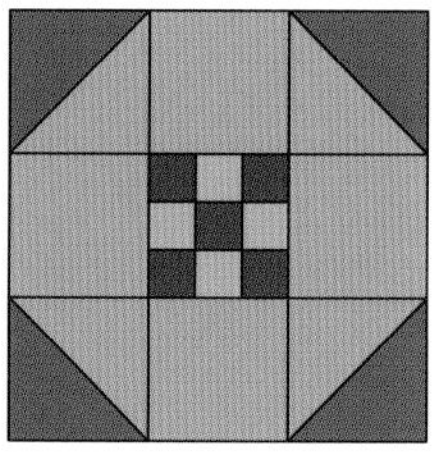
Block 6: Make 1.

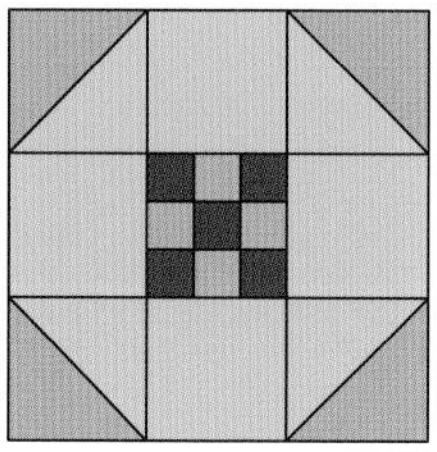
Block 7: Make 1.

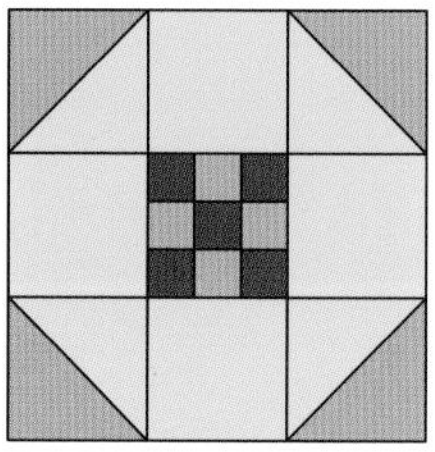
Block 8: Make 1.

Assembly

STEP 1 Lay out the 16 blocks in 4 rows of 4 blocks each. Make sure the blocks with the hot pink edges are on the left side and the 3 green blocks are on the bottom row on the right side.

4	1	1	1
3	2	1	1
3	1	1	2
5	6	7	8

Block layout

STEP 2 Sew the blocks together in rows first, and then join the rows.

Quilt assembly

Finishing

Refer to Finishing the Quilt (page 12) as needed.

Layer and baste the quilt.

QUILTING

While the term *poppy* brings to mind curvy, floral designs, using a geometric quilting design is an unexpected option that can look stunning. The dot-to-dot quilting method, which uses points on the blocks to create a multifaceted design, is perfect for these big, beautiful blocks.

Dot to Dot

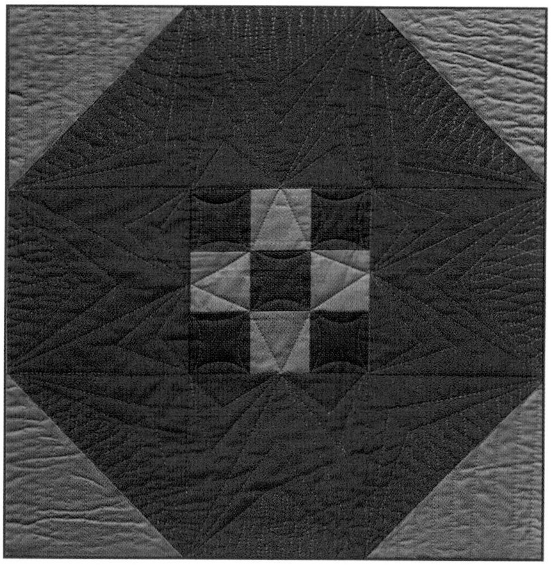

While you may have already seen designs with diagonal lines in this book, this design takes it up a step by combining diagonal lines with free-motion quilting.

STEP 1 Starting at the upper left corner of the Nine-Patch, quilt a line that goes directly up to the edge of the block, down to the midpoint, and up to the outer edge. *Fig. A*

STEP 2 Quilt a line that echoes the triangle, and then quilt the wishbone design, returning to the upper right point. *Fig. B*

Tip

You can use any filler you like, such as back-and-forth lines or a meander.

STEP 3 Quilt another line down to the upper right corner of the Nine-Patch block. Quilt diagonal lines echoing the shape out to the starting point and back again. *Fig. C*

STEP 4 Quilt a horizontal line to the right edge of the block. Echo the shape, and then quilt a wishbone design, returning to the edge of the block. *Fig. D*

STEP 5 Repeat this process, working your way around the blocks and going from point to point. *Fig. E*

STEP 6 You've reached the original starting point and need to finish the last half-square triangle. From here, backtrack along the very first line of stitching, and then quilt diagonal lines over to left side of the block; then add the last filler design. *Fig. F*

STEP 7 Finish the block by stitching a V along the bottom of all the filler designs, defining the area. *Fig. G*

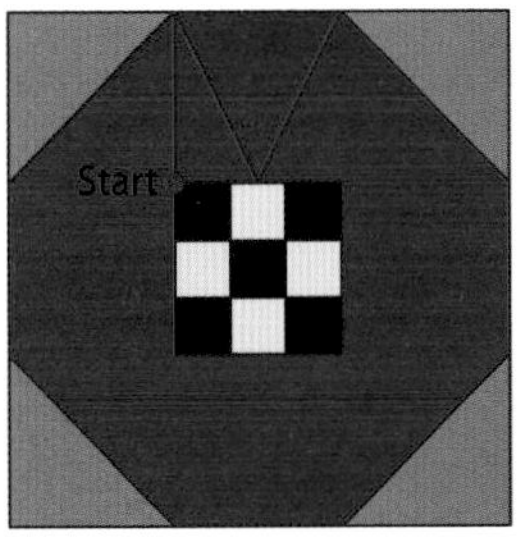

A

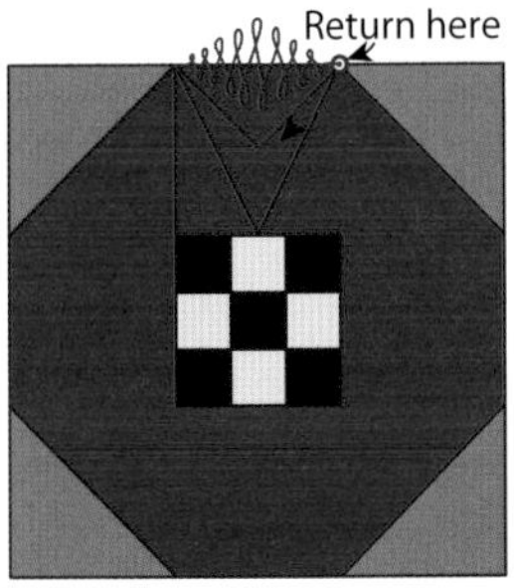

B

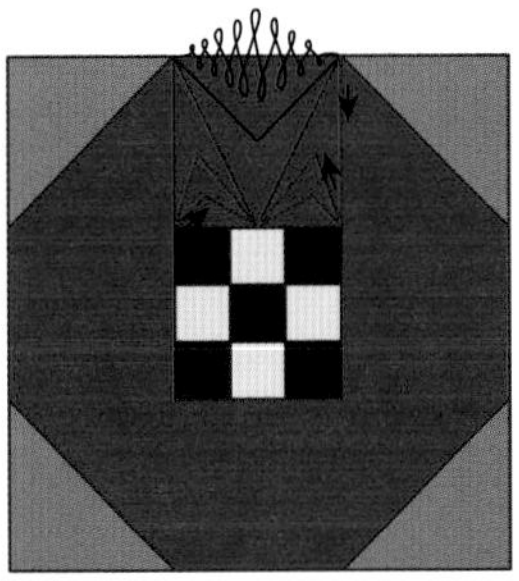

C

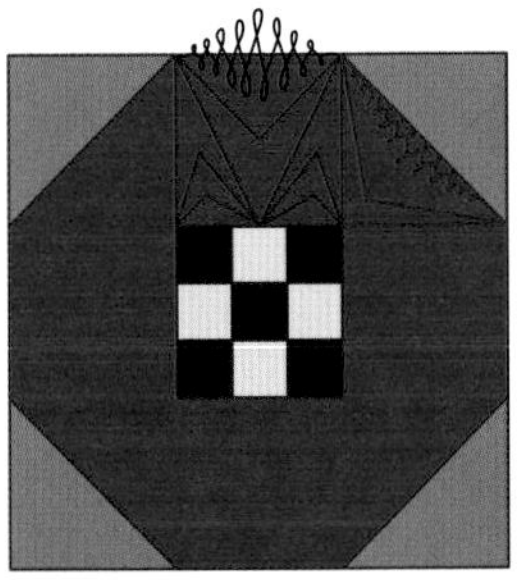

D

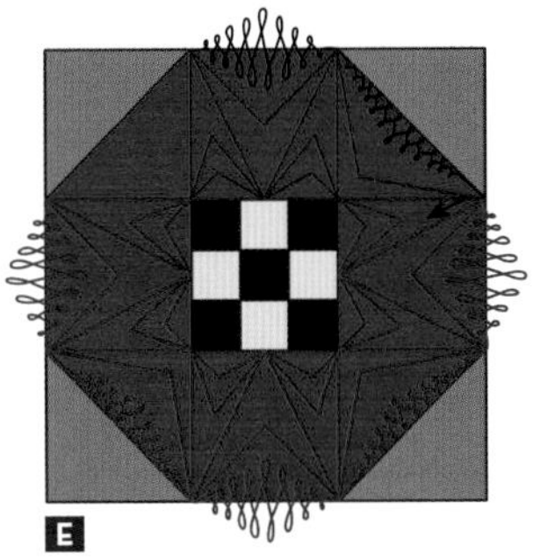

E

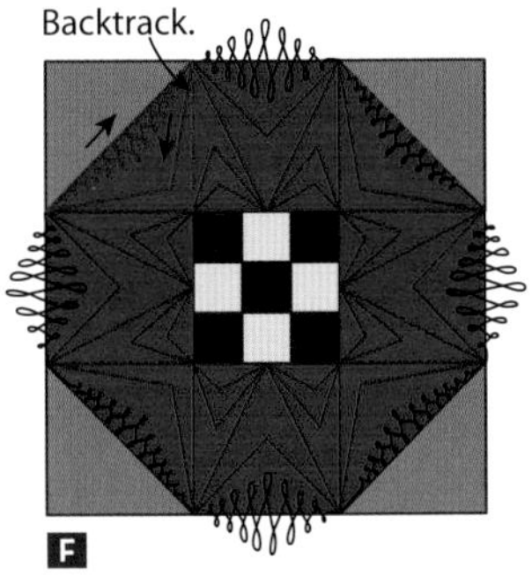

F

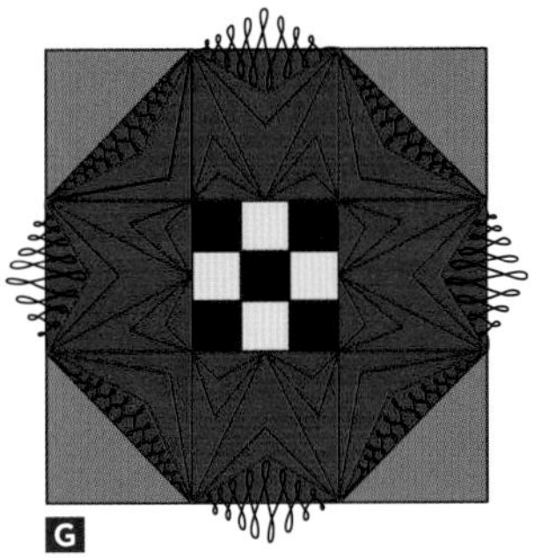

G

THE LAST STEP

Add the binding to your quilt, referring to Binding (page 14) as needed. Note that *Poppy: A Modern Reproduction* requires about 375″ of binding.

NOTE

If this seems like too much effort, you can skip all the straight lines and quilt swirls in the block. It will also look great!

Wasabi Bomb

FINISHED QUILT: 81″ × 81″ ■ FINISHED BLOCK: 27″ × 27″

Optical illusions and quilts just go together (see full quilt, page 104)! This Log Cabin-style block can be set together in a variety of ways to take advantage of the unsteadying effects of the block.

Design Notes

Any two colors work great—just make sure there is high contrast so the optical illusion shows.

Fabrics

Yardage is based on 42″ usable fabric width. WOF = width of fabric.

Green solid: 3 5/8 yards

White: 3 5/8 yards

Binding: 3/4 yard green or white

Backing: 7 1/2 yards

Batting: 87″ × 87″

Cutting

WHITE

Cut 23 strips 3 1/2″ × WOF.

Cut 30 strips 1 1/2″ × WOF.

GREEN

Cut 22 strips 3 1/2″ × WOF.

Cut 30 strips 1 1/2″ × WOF.

BINDING

Cut 9 strips 2 1/2″ × WOF.

Blocks

Use a ¼″ seam allowance. Refer to Strip-Set Construction (page 11) as needed.

NINE-PATCH BLOCKS

STEP 1 Using 2 green 1½″ × WOF strips and 1 white 1½″ × WOF strip, make a green / white / green strip set (Strip Set 1).

STEP 2 Using 2 white 1½″ × WOF strips and 1 green 1½″ × WOF strip, make the second white / green / white strip set (Strip Set 2).

STEP 3 Cut Strip Set 1 into 13 units 1½″ wide and Strip Set 2 into 14 units 1½″ wide. Piece together the Nine-Patches—make 5 Nine-Patches with white corners (Nine-Patch A) and 4 Nine-Patches with green corners (Nine-Patch B).

Nine-Patch A:
3½″ × 3½″

Nine-Patch B:
3½″ × 3½″

BLOCKS A AND B

These blocks are made Log Cabin–style, starting with a Nine-Patch in the center.

Block Cutting Chart

Subcut the 1½″ and 3½″ × WOF strips as indicated in both green and white fabrics for Blocks A and B. For example, in the first row of the chart, 5 white 1½″ strips will be cut into 10½″ and 27½″ lengths for Block A; 4 strips will be cut to those lengths in green for Block B. Keep the strips organized by block and in order of length. This will help the piecing process.

	First cut	Second cut	Third cut	Number of WOF white strips for Blocks A and B	Number of WOF green strips for Blocks A and B
1½″ strips	10½″	27½″	–	5A	4B
	11½″	26½″	–	5A	4B
	18½″	19½	–	5A	4B
	6½″	23½″	–	4B	5A
	7½″	22½″	–	4B	5A
	14½″	15½″	–	4B	5A
3½″ strips	7½″	26½″	–	5A	4B
	10½″	23½″	–	5A	4B
	15½″	18½″	–	5A	4B
	3½″	11½″	22½″	4B	5A
	6½″	14½″	19½″	4B	5A

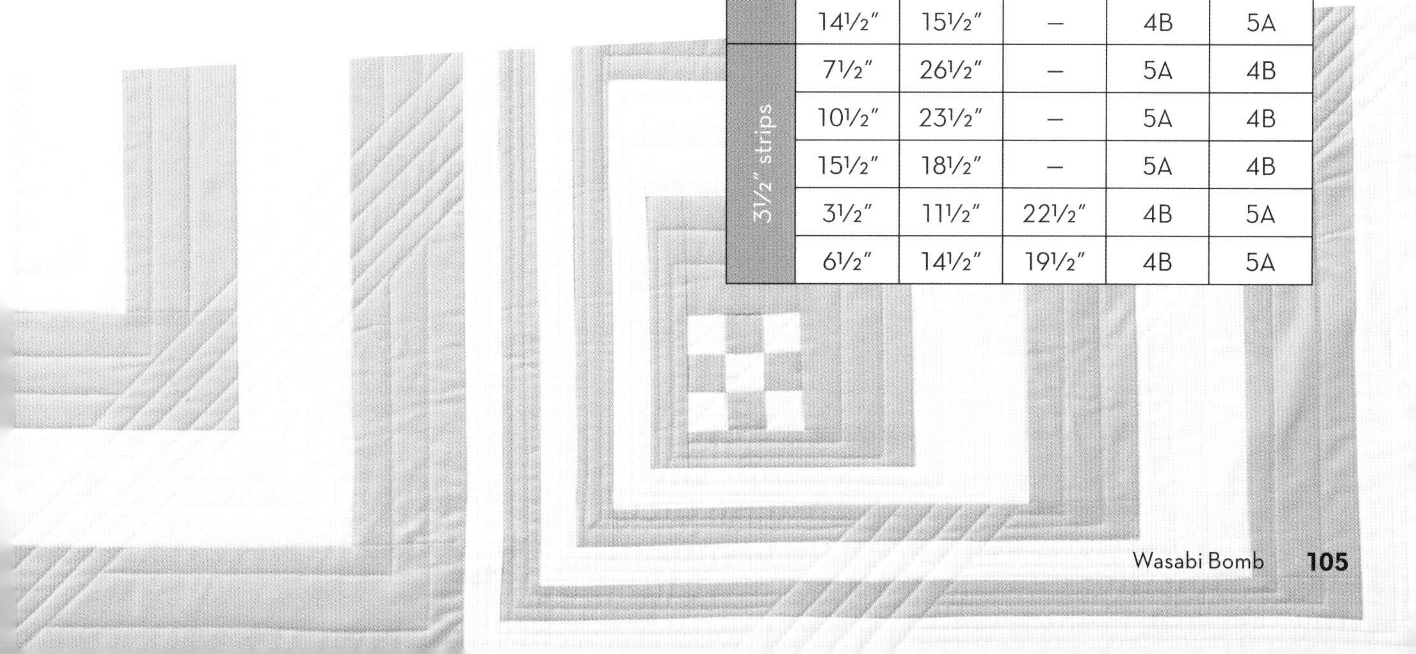

Block Construction Chart

Both blocks are sewn beginning on the right hand side of the center Nine-Patch, adding one strip to a side moving clockwise around. The only difference between the 2 blocks is the color of the strip sewn in the sequence. The size of the strips in the sequence remains the same in both blocks. Plus the pattern remains constant: Add 2 wide strips, 2 narrow strips; 4 of one color, 4 of the next.

For the position of each strip within the block, refer to the Block A and Block B diagrams (below) and the chart (next page).

BLOCK A

Sew a Nine-Patch A to the green 3½″ × 3½″ square (1). Press toward the green. Sew the 3½″ × 6½″ green rectangle (2) to the bottom of this unit with the Nine-Patch on the left. Press toward the green. Sew the 1½″ × 6½″ green strip (3) to the left of this unit. End the first round by sewing the 1½″ × 7½″ green strip (4) to the top. Switch to white strips in the second round.

Continue sewing in numerical order, following the Block A diagram and the chart. Make 5 blocks 27½″ × 27½″ *unfinished.*

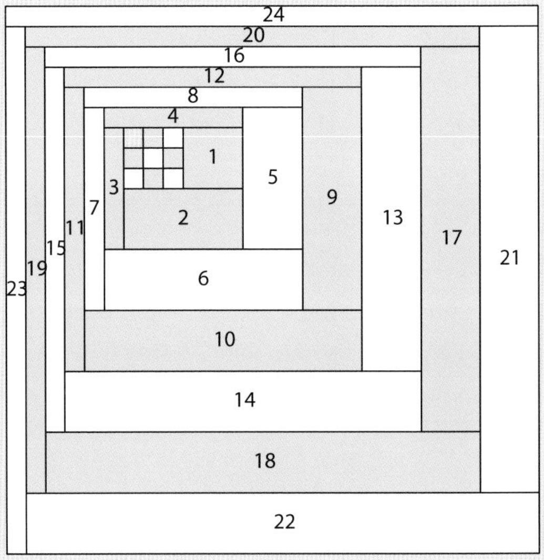

Block A: 27½″ × 27½″

BLOCK B

Block B uses the opposite color of Block A. Sew a Nine-Patch B to the white 3½″ × 3½″ square (1). Press toward the Nine-Patch. Sew the 3½″ × 6½″ white rectangle (2) to the bottom of this unit with the Nine-Patch on the left. Press toward the Nine-Patch. Sew the 1½″ × 6½″ white strip (3) to the left of this unit. End the first round by sewing the 1½″ × 7½″ white strip (4) to the top. Switch to green for the next round.

Continue sewing in numerical order, following the Block B diagram and the chart. Make 4 blocks 27½″ × 27½″ *unfinished.*

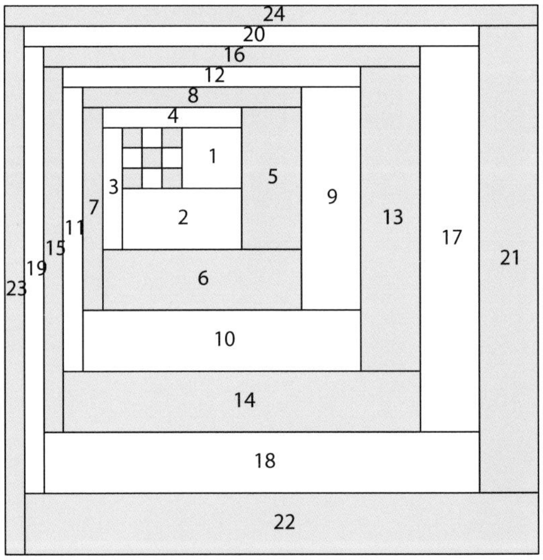

Block B: 27½″ × 27½″

Block position	Cut size	Block A	Block B
1	3½″ × 3½″	GR	WH
2	3½″ × 6½″	GR	WH
3	1½″ × 6½″	GR	WH
4	1½″ × 7½″	GR	WH
5	3½″ × 7½″	WH	GR
6	3½″ × 10½″	WH	GR
7	1½″ × 10½″	WH	GR
8	1½″ × 11½″	WH	GR
9	3½″ × 11½″	GR	WH
10	3½″ × 14½″	GR	WH
11	1½″ × 14½″	GR	WH
12	1½″ × 15½″	GR	WH
13	3½″ × 15½″	WH	GR
14	3½″ × 18½″	WH	GR
15	1½″ × 18½″	WH	GR
16	1½″ × 19½″	WH	GR
17	3½″ × 19½″	GR	WH
18	3½″ × 22½″	GR	WH
19	1½″ × 22½″	GR	WH
20	1½″ × 23½″	GR	WH
21	3½″ × 23½″	WH	GR
22	3½″ × 26½″	WH	GR
23	1½″ × 26½″	WH	GR
24	1½″ × 27½″	WH	GR

Assembly

STEP 1 Lay out the 9 blocks in 3 rows of 3 blocks each. Using a design wall or the floor, experiment with different placements.

STEP 2 Sew the blocks together into rows, and then join the rows.

Quilt assembly

Finishing

Refer to Finishing the Quilt (page 12) as needed.

Layer and baste the quilt.

QUILTING

To keep the optical illusion created by the piecing going, try using straight lines that highlight the difference in spacing between the sides of the blocks. It shows that quilting can be easy and impactful.

Echoing the Nine-Patch

To make this design as easy as possible, use the piecing as a guide for the lines. If you are quilting on a sewing machine, you can use a walking foot to help keep the lines straight.

STEP 1 After quilting the center Nine-Patch, quilt a line that extends 1/4″ from the bottom corner. Echo around the whole block in a squared spiral, quilting the lines in the skinnier parts of the block closer together than the lines in the wider part of the block. Once the area is filled, extend into the next "ring" of the block by 1/4″. *Fig. A*

STEP 2 Continue echoing around the block, working your way toward the outer ring of the block. *Fig. B*

Tip

Don't worry about the amount of spacing between the lines. In fact, it might look better if it's more random.

Breaking It Up

If you're having trouble with the longer lines around the outside of the block, you can use diagonal lines to break up the area. This is especially helpful if you are quilting on a longarm machine.

You don't have to tell anyone that you quilted the diagonal lines to make it easier! Just say that you did it for artistic reasons. I won't tell if you won't!

THE LAST STEP

Add the binding to your quilt, referring to Binding (page 14) as needed. Note that *Wasabi Bomb* requires about 340″ of binding.

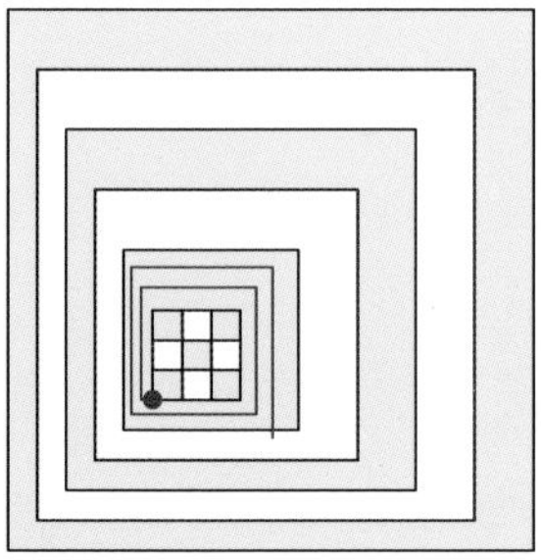

A

B

The Importance of Being Pink

FINISHED QUILT: 93˝ × 87˝ ■ FINISHED BLOCK: 18˝ × 36˝

Don't be afraid of bold color choices—not every quilt has to match your decor! This color palette is 1970s inspired, but you could easily change the three colors to anything you like.

Design Notes

The large scale of the blocks makes this a statement piece worthy of hanging on the wall!

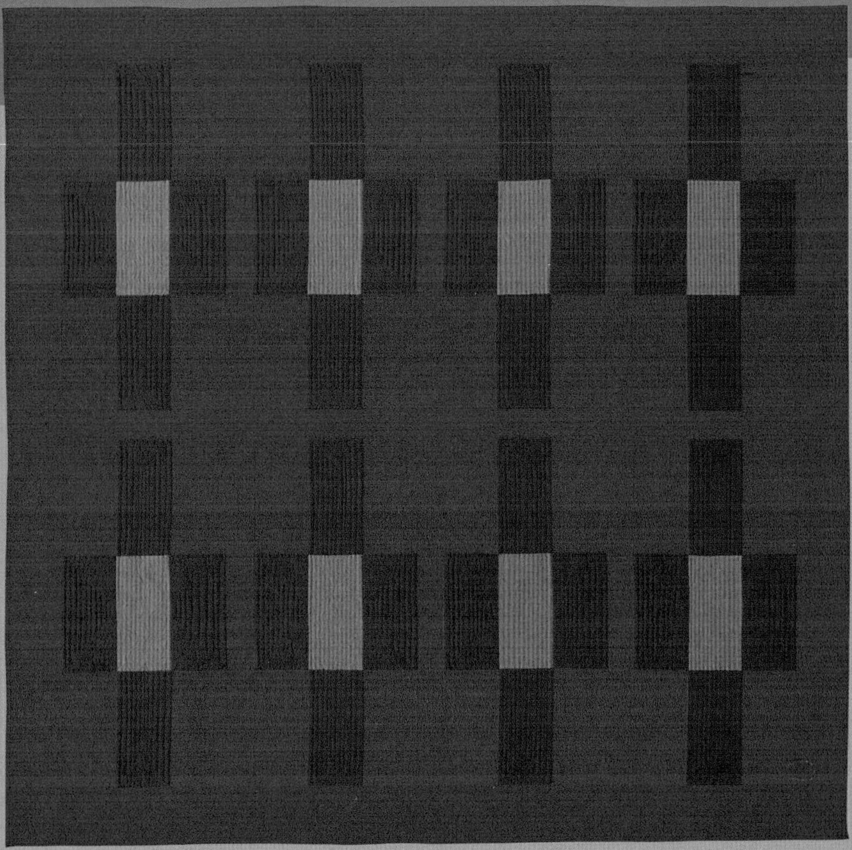

Fabrics

Yardage is based on 42″ usable fabric width. WOF = width of fabric.

Pink: 5½ yards

Red: 2¼ yards

Orange: ¾ yard

Backing: 8 yards

Batting: 99″ × 93″

Cutting

PINK

Blocks:

Cut 11 strips 6½″ × WOF; subcut 32 rectangles 6½″ × 12½″.

Sashing:

Cut 6 strips 3½″ × 36½″ for vertical sashing.

Cut 2 strips 3½″ × WOF for horizontal sashing.

Binding:

Cut 9 strips 2½″ × WOF.

Borders:

Cut 9 strips 6½″ × WOF.

RED

Cut 11 strips 6½″ × WOF; subcut 32 rectangles 6½″ × 12½″.

ORANGE

Cut 3 strips 6½″ × WOF; subcut 8 rectangles 6½″ × 12½″.

Blocks

Use a ¼″ seam allowance. Refer to Basic Construction (page 8) as needed.

Each block uses 4 pink, 4 red, and 1 orange rectangle; make 8 Nine-Patch blocks.

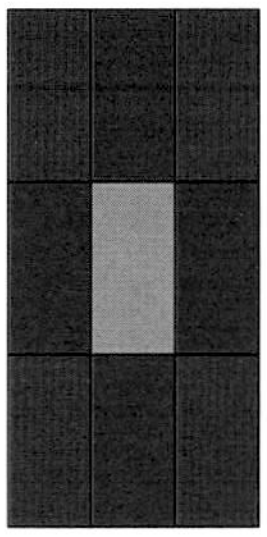

18½″ × 36½″

Assembly

SASHING

STEP 1 Refer to the quilt assembly diagram to sew 3 vertical sashing strips between 4 Nine-Patch blocks. Press toward the sashing.

STEP 2 Repeat with the remaining sashing strips and blocks to make 2 rows.

STEP 3 Piece together the 2 remaining 3½″ × WOF sashing strips. Measure the rows and average the number if they aren't the same. Cut the sashing strip to this length.

STEP 4 Sew the rows to the center sashing strip, making sure to align the blocks as you do.

BORDERS

STEP 1 Piece together the 9 border strips 6½″ × WOF into 1 long length. Cut 2 strips the same length as the center sashing strip.

STEP 2 Sew the strips to the top and bottom of the quilt.

STEP 3 Measure the quilt from top to bottom through the middle and cut 2 strips this length.

STEP 4 Sew the strips to the sides of the quilt.

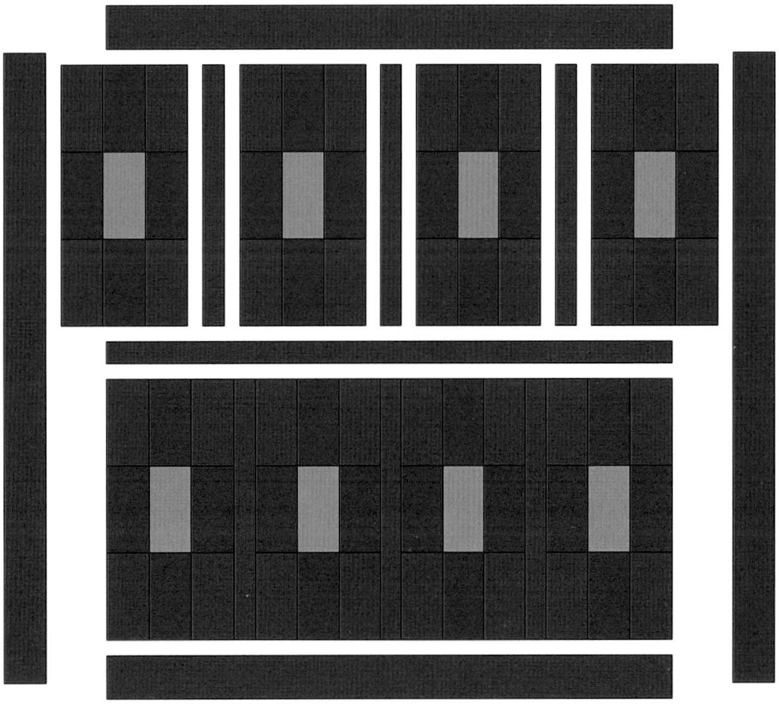

Quilt assembly

Finishing

Refer to Finishing the Quilt (page 12) as needed.

Layer and baste the quilt.

QUILTING

A quilt made up of big blocks means that there is so much more area for you to have fun quilting. Alternating between a few different designs can be an impressive way to finish up this big, beautiful pink quilt.

In the Blocks

Start off simply by quilting straight lines that echo the piecing. This is a great way to highlight the blocks and really make them the focal point of the quilt. Try echoing just the 4 red blocks on each side of the orange center with ¼″–½″ spacing between lines—it'll look great!

In the Background

Since the area is so large, you can use two different designs in the background. Quilting elegant paisley feathers surrounded by wavy lines is a combination worthy of such a gorgeous quilt.

Wavy lines

Paisley feathers

PAISLEY FEATHER

STEP 1 Quilt an elongated swirl and echo it around the outside 3 more times, ending at the bottom of the swirl.

STEP 2 Quilt a thin tear-dropped shaped paisley that extends from the swirl and echo around it a few more times, ending between the paisley and the swirl.

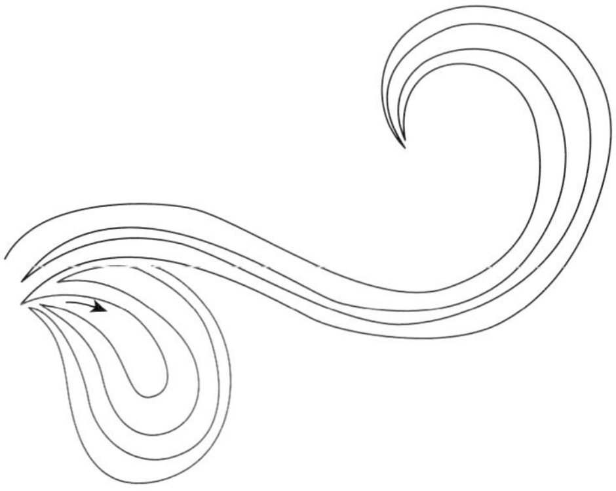

STEP 3 Continue quilting echoed paisleys, working around to the center of the swirl. Echo around the whole paisley until you reach the area where you want to quilt the next one.

Tip

The bigger the feather is, the better it looks. Don't be afraid to make the feathers nice and large. Not only will it look better, but it will also make the quilting go faster. Talk about a win/win!

THE LAST STEP

Add the binding to your quilt, referring to Binding (page 14) as needed. Note that *The Importance of Being Pink* requires about 375″ of binding.

Color Columns

FINISHED QUILT: 81″ × 90″ ■ FINISHED BLOCK: 9″ × 9″

Color Columns is an organized scrap quilt that puts your stash to good use! Each column is made of a single color family. The length of the pieced column depends on how much of a particular color you have in your stash. No two quilts are the same!

Design Notes

Gather all your scraps before you start making the Nine-Patches. The longest columns will be the color that you have the most of in your stash! My columns range from 2 to 9 Nine-Patch blocks; each Nine-Patch consists of 2 fabrics.

Fabrics

Yardage is based on 42″ usable fabric width. WOF = width of fabric.

Light to medium gray: 3¼ yards for background and binding

Assorted prints and solids: 9 color families in a wide variety of values
Each Nine-Patch block uses 2 different fabrics: 2 scraps (at least 1 rectangle 8″ × 11″ and 1 square 8″ × 8″) or 2 fat eighths. (See Fabric Note, below.)

Coordinating print: 7½ yards for backing

Batting: 87″ × 96″

FABRIC NOTE

For the assorted prints and solids, use a wide variety of values and try not to repeat fabrics within each color except within the block. Each Nine-Patch is made of 3½″ × 3½″ squares: 5 from one fabric (8″ × 11″ scrap) and 4 from another (8″ × 8″ scrap).

Look through your scraps first, then fill in with purchased fat eighths, if necessary.

In order to avoid repeating fabrics, count the number of Nine-Patch blocks in a color column and double that for the number of fabrics you need in that colorway. For instance, if you choose column 3 as your green colorway, you will need 8 greens for 4 Nine-Patches. In total there are 52 pairs of fabrics.

Column 1: 14	**Column 4:** 10	**Column 7:** 14
Column 2: 4	**Column 5:** 18	**Column 8:** 8
Column 3: 8	**Column 6:** 12	**Column 9:** 16

Cutting

GRAY

Sashing:

Cut 9 strips 9½″ × WOF.

Binding:

Cut 9 strips 2½″ × WOF.

Blocks

Use a 1/4″ seam allowance. Refer to Basic Construction (page 8) as needed.

Determine 2 fabrics for each block. Make most with low contrast between the darker and lighter fabric and some with high contrast. This will avoid a strong checkerboard look to the columns. The goal is for the fabrics to blend throughout the whole column.

Cut 9 total squares 3½″ × 3½″ for each block—5 squares of one print and 4 squares of another print.

Make the number of Nine-Patches per column as shown in the quilt assembly diagram (below) or the number of Nine-Patches according to the color-way scraps you have in your stash.

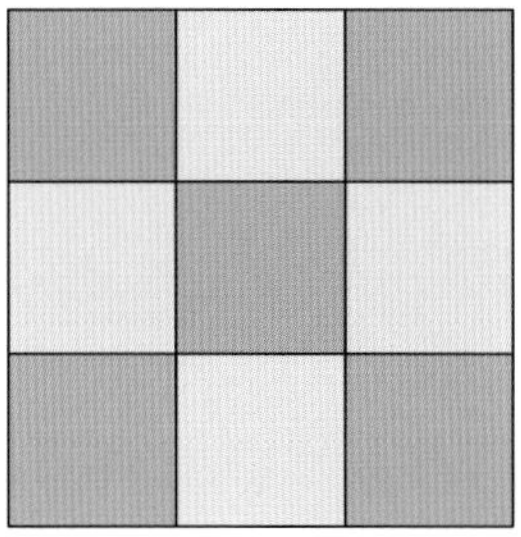

9½″ × 9½″

Assembly

Each column is 9½″ × 90½″. My version of *Color Columns* has cool colors flanked by warm colors. Your arrangement may be different depending on what colors you used for each column. For the most interest, be sure to stagger the columns so they aren't all placed lowest to tallest.

Piece the gray 9½″ × WOF strips together into 1 long strip; subcut into the lengths, shown in the quilt assembly diagram or to the length you need, to make your columns equal to 90½″. Sew each pieced Nine-Patch column to its corresponding gray strip. Join the columns.

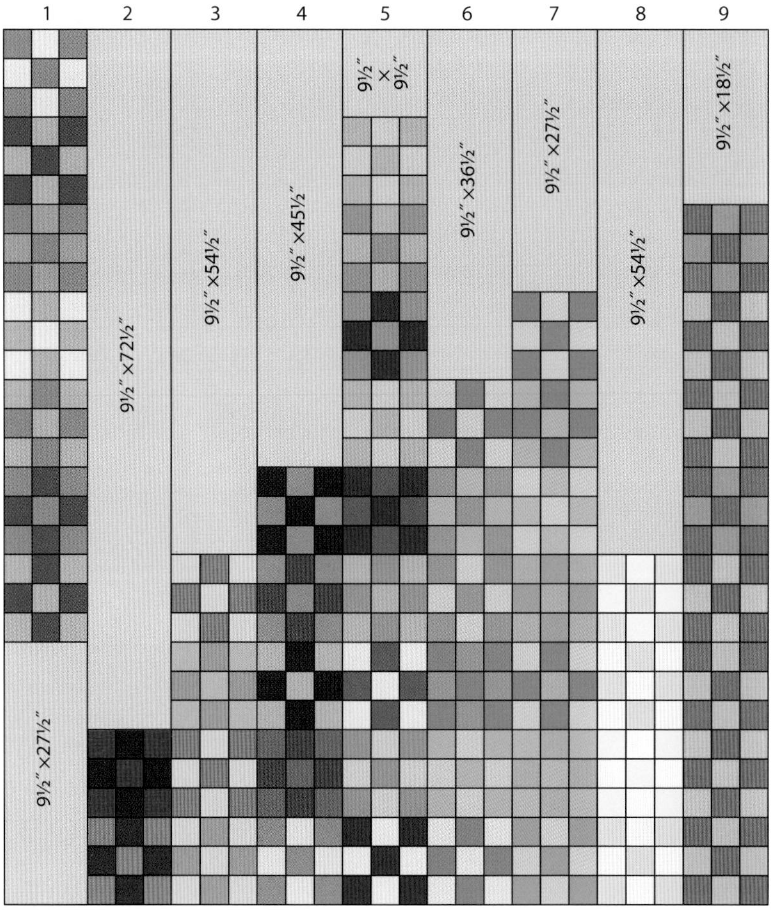

Quilt assembly

Finishing

Refer to Finishing the Quilt (page 12) as needed.

Layer and baste the quilt.

QUILTING

Stacks of bright colors are the perfect foundation for some fun quilting, especially in the large areas of background space. You can add interest to theses areas using relatively straight lines and free-motion quilting designs without taking away from the beautiful colors of the fabrics.

Continuous curves (page 13) in the Nine-Patch columns

Merged Lines with Filler

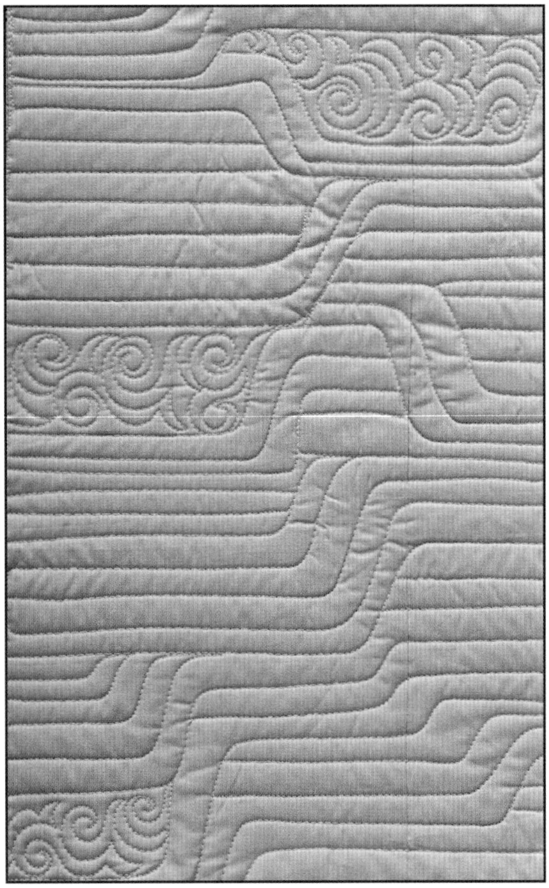

NOTE

This design is easier to quilt in areas of background space that are about 8″–12″ apart. Once you get the hang of quilting it, you can try it in larger (or smaller) areas.

STEP 1 Starting on one side of the quilting area, quilt a horizontal line toward the opposite side. At a random point, angle down (or in the direction you are heading) and then return to quilting a horizontal line until you run into the edge. *Fig. A*

STEP 2 Travel along the seam about ½″, and then quilt another horizontal line back to the other side. As you did in Step 1, angle down at a random point and then resume the horizontal line until you reach the other side. *Fig. B*

Tip

You can quilt the line so that it angles down as much or as little as you'd like. It's completely up to you!

STEP 3 Travel up along the edge ½″ and echo the line until you run into the top line. *Fig. C*

STEP 4 Continue echoing and traveling until the space between the lines is filled in. Be sure to end on the edge of the quilting area. *Fig. D*

STEP 5 Travel along the edge until you are ½″ below the last line of the design. As you did in Step 1, quilt a horizontal line that angles down at a random point and then evens out. Travel up along the edge ½″ and echo the line until you run into the previously quilted line. *Fig. E*

STEP 6 Start quilting a free-motion quilting design, such as swirls, filling in the unquilted area and working out to the edge. *Fig. F*

STEP 7 Travel down along the edge about ½″ below the last quilted line on that side and repeat Steps 1–4. *Fig. G*

Tip

To achieve a random look with the quilting, alternate between echo lines or free-motion quilting filler. Keep experimenting until you find what looks great to you!

STEP 8 Continue quilting, repeating Steps 1–7 until the whole area is completely filled in. *Fig. H*

NOTE

If you run into the top (or bottom) of an area, just echo the main line traveling along to the edge. The most important thing is that you fill in the area. Even if it isn't perfect, it won't be as noticeable as a gap in the quilting.

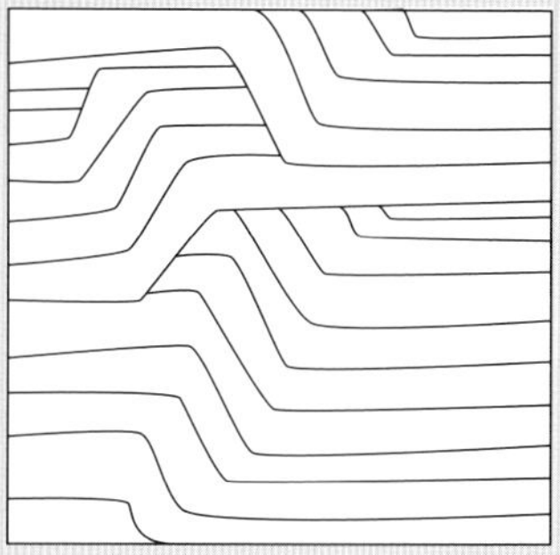

Use echoing to fill in areas above or below design.

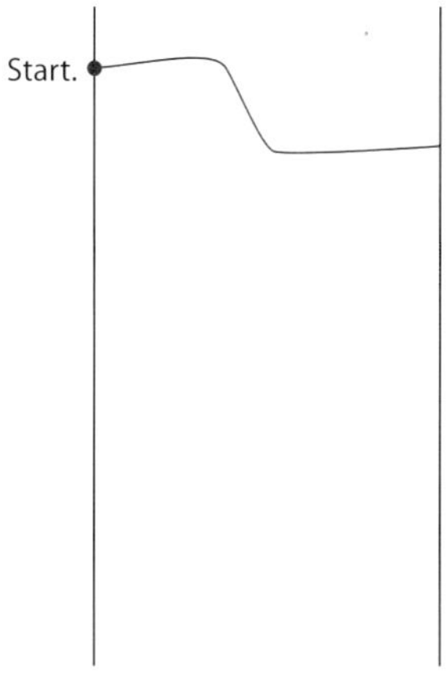

A

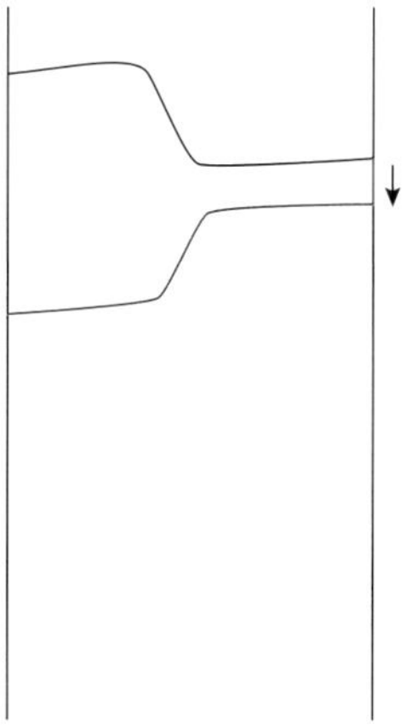

B

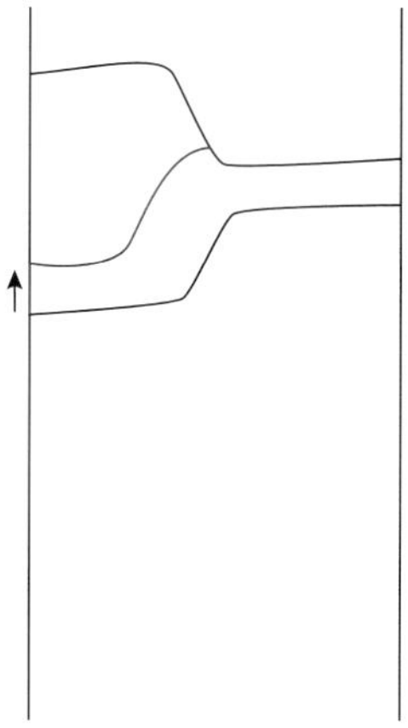

C

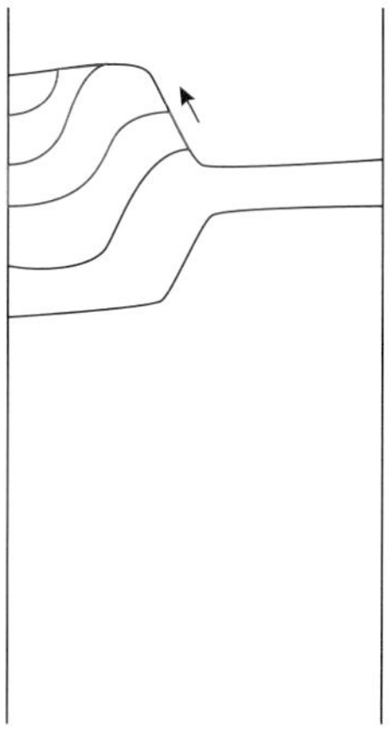

D

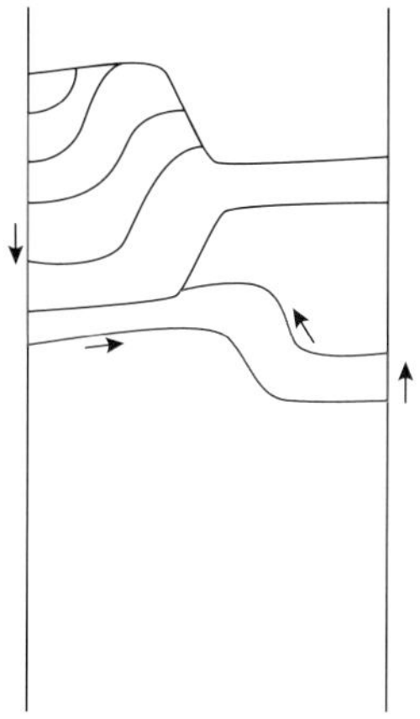

E

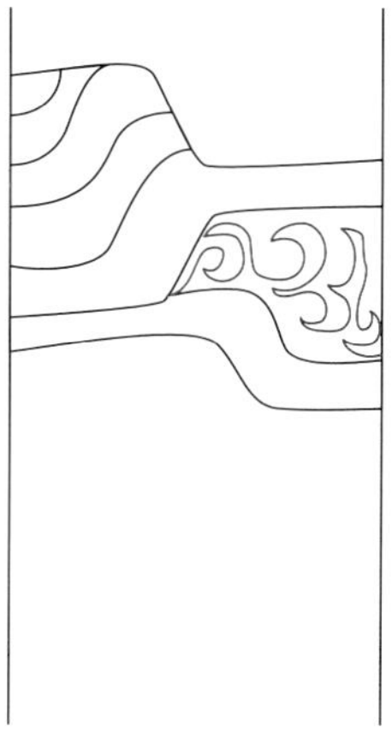

F

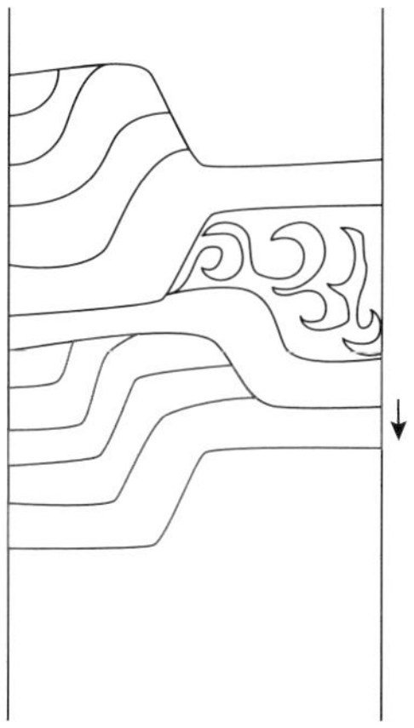

G

H

THE LAST STEP

Add the binding to your quilt, referring to Binding (page 14) as needed. Note that *Color Columns* requires about 360″ of binding.

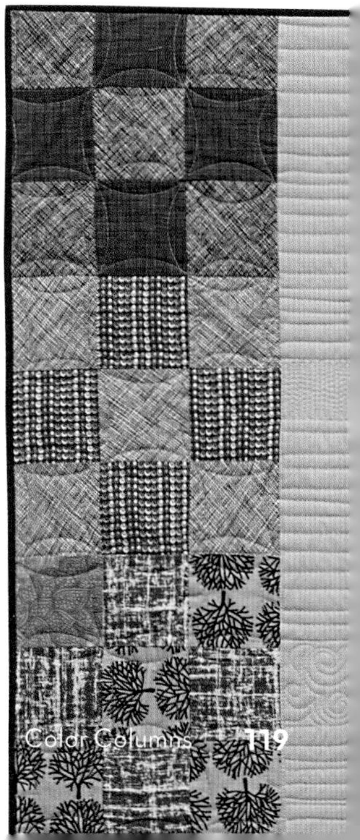

Medallion

FINISHED QUILT: 78″ × 78″ ■ FINISHED BLOCK: 6″ × 6″

Antique quilts are a continual source of inspiration. The beauty that comes from making do is hard to recreate, but it can be done! To make your *Medallion* quilt in the vintage, make-do style, use only fabrics in your stash, and when you run out of one, continue with another. Often the improvised version is better than the planned!

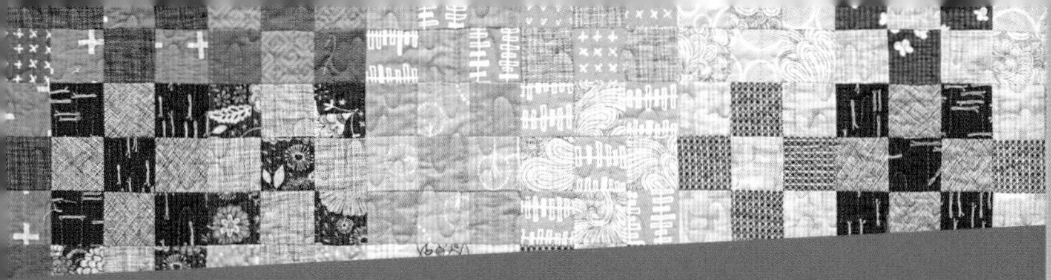

Design Notes

Look through your stash and pick out two or three colorways that look good together. Pick lights, mediums, and darks of each print. Throw in an oddball to keep it interesting!

Fabrics

Yardage is based on 42″ usable fabric width. WOF = width of fabric.

Since this quilt is improv-pieced, you determine how much of each fabric and what colors you use as you piece the Nine-Patches. Start by determining the constant color. In this case, gray is the constant. Each block uses a light, medium, or dark gray print, with the darker grays on the outside of the quilt and the lighter grays toward the center.

Gather the fabrics from your stash. Pick 2 accents that you think look good together *and* that you have the most of in your stash. In this case, the 2 accent colors are gradations of pink to burgundy and aqua to teal.

For the oddball fabric, now is a good chance to use that fabric you bought on a whim and later regretted, or that you bought for another project that will never be made! In this case, the oddball is red.

Try to pick prints that have different scales. Some should read as solids even though there is some texture to the print and some can be larger-scale with other colors in it. That makes the quilt more blended and less stark from block to block.

Constant color: 5/8–3/4 yard each of roughly 5 gradations of the same color for a total of 3 3/8 yards

Accent 1: 1/3–3/8 yard each of roughly 5 gradations of the same color for a total of 1 3/4 yards

Accent 2: 1/3–3/8 yard each of roughly 5 gradations of the same color for a total of 1 3/4 yards

Oddball fabric: 3/8–1/2 yard of a print shockingly different from the accent fabrics

Binding: 5/8 yard gray print

Batting: 84″ × 84″

Backing: Because this quilt needs 2″ more in length and width to accommodate longarm quilting, it would be economical to purchase 5 yards of backing and add 1 1/2″–2″ strips of muslin or other scrap fabric to all sides to extend the quilting allowance.

Cutting

CONSTANT COLOR

Cut a total of 48 strips 2½″ × WOF; subcut 768 squares 2½″ × 2½″.

ACCENT FABRIC 1

Cut a total of 22 strips 2½″ × WOF; subcut 352 squares 2½″ × 2½″.

ACCENT FABRIC 2

Cut a total of 22 strips 2½″ × WOF; subcut 352 squares 2½″ × 2½″.

ODDBALL FABRIC

Cut 5 strips 2½″ × WOF; subcut 80 squares 2½″ × 2½″.

> NOTE
>
> If you need to purchase fabric, keep in mind that you can get 56 squares 2½″ × 2½″ from 1 fat quarter. This yields 14 blocks using 4 of the same squares or 11 blocks using 5 of the same squares. For most fabrics, you will only need fat quarters, but for some you will need half-yard cuts.

Blocks

Use a ¼″ seam allowance. Refer to Basic Construction (page 8) as needed.

6½″ × 6½″

The quilt is made of 169 blocks in a 13 × 13 grid. It is made symmetrically in 4 identical quadrants.

The blocks are 6½″ × 6½″ *unfinished* and are made of 2½″ × 2½″ squares with the seams pressed open.

Start making Nine-Patches with the two fabrics you have the most of. This will determine the center of the quilt. Experiment with placement of the colors within each block—and, once pieced, the placement of the blocks. Some unexpected options will pop up for the center medallion if you experiment with a lot of different layouts.

Once you determine the center medallion, work out from there. It's easiest to work with one quadrant at a time, making adjustments and changes as you go. As you make decisions, piece the blocks for the other three quadrants.

If you run out of fabric, either use something almost identical or swap out the blocks completely for another color combination and use the swapped blocks in another way. Often what you think will work ends up working better when used differently!

Tips

- *Press all the seams open so they join together easily when piecing the top together.*
- *Each block is made of only two fabrics, a constant color and an accent color. Not all have to be made of nine squares, however. Making some with crosses (as seen in the center and corners of the quilt) make for more interesting placement options.*
- *Make some blocks with the constant color on the outer corners and some with the accents on the outer corners. This gives it more variety and avoids a strong checkerboard look. It is okay if constant color touches constant color or accent touches accent.*
- *Keep value in mind when determining placement. You want the light and dark to flow over the top of the quilt. This will highlight some areas and make other areas recede.*
- *Take pictures of different layout options so you can remember what you like and eliminate what you don't. Also, when you determine your final placement, take a picture so you have a reference to keep you from getting lost as you piece together the quadrants.*

NOTE

If you don't want a symmetrical layout for your quilt, a random placement is another fun option. There are no decisions other than the two fabrics you choose for each block—a constant color and an accent, or a constant color and an oddball. You don't have to think about how many of each to make, and you can just keep going until the fabric runs out, then start with another two fabrics! Joining the blocks together randomly gives it an old-fashioned feel.

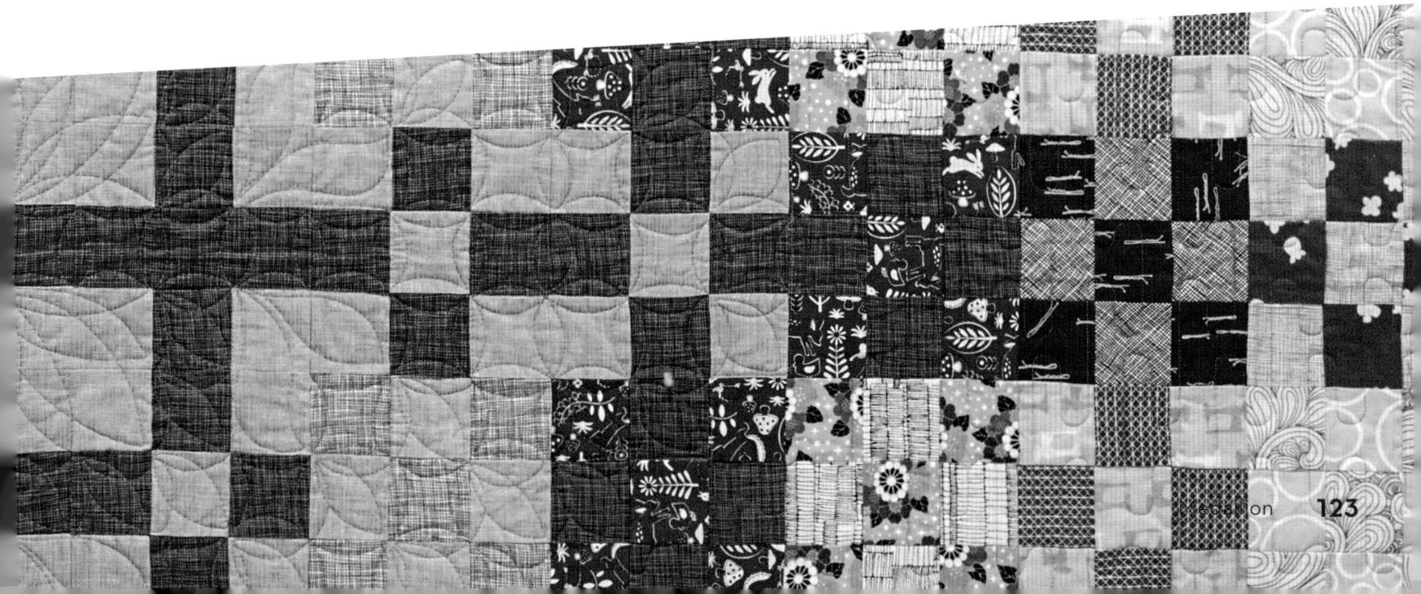

Assembly

Referring to the quilt assembly diagram, piece together 1 quadrant in a panel of 6 × 6 blocks and use that as a reference for the other 3. Piece the 4 center rows and the very center block to the quadrants, and then join them together.

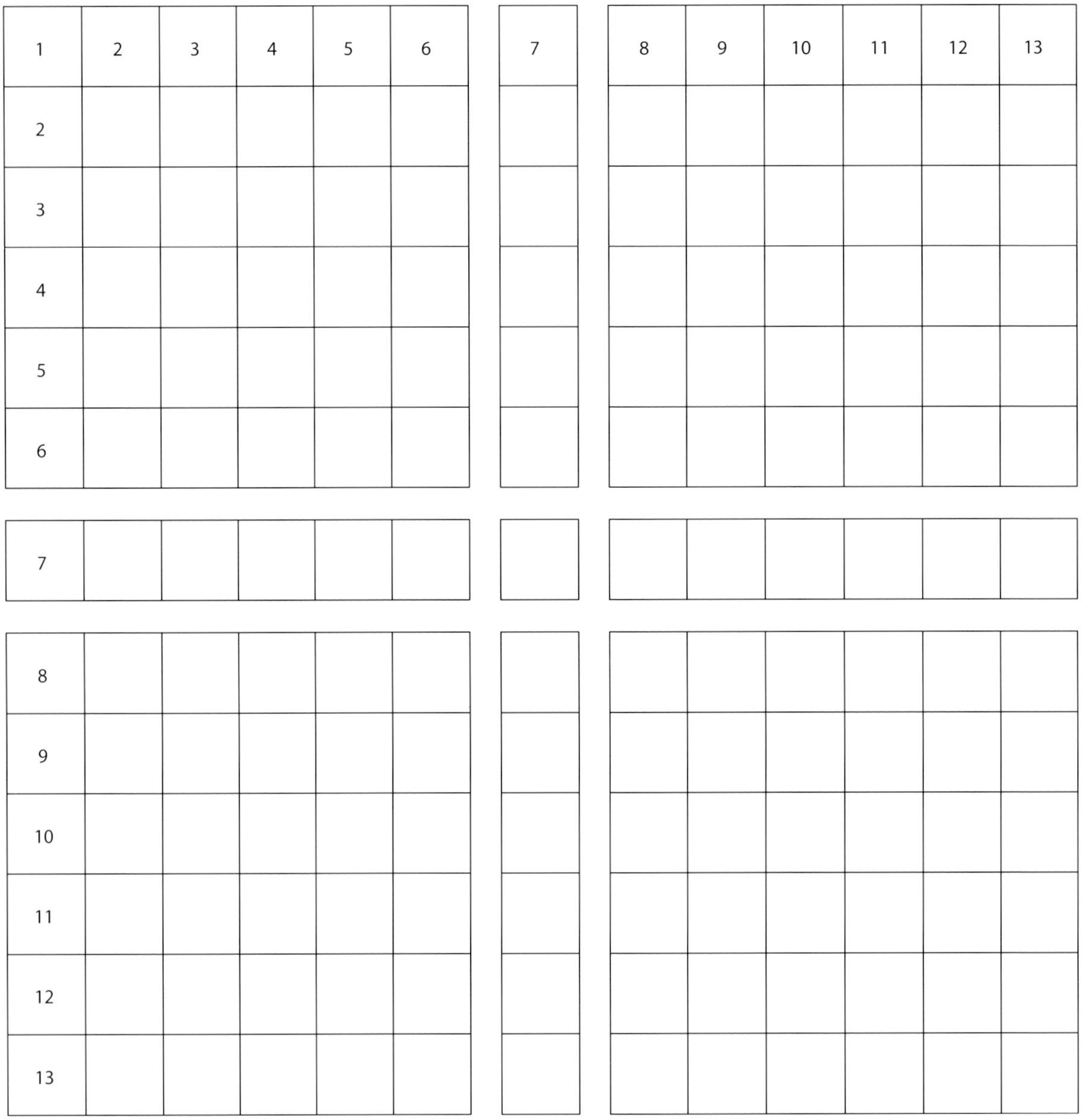

Quilt assembly

Finishing

Refer to Finishing the Quilt (page 12) as needed.

Layer and baste the quilt.

QUILTING

Every once in awhile you'll come across a quilt like *Medallion*, in which *what* you quilt isn't as important as *how* you quilt it. The pink blocks in the center of this quilt really shine from the rest of the piecing. Quilting the designs so that they radiate from the center of the quilt further helps draw the eye there.

Even though the leaves and flowered curves quilted in *Medallion* are fairly basic, they create an almost medallion-like effect in themselves when they are oriented around the center.

Continuous Curve Leaves

Tip

The leaves don't have to be perfect or symmetrical. Just try to make them fill in the block as much as possible and it will look great.

This design, using continuous curves (page 13) allows you to start and stop at the same point, making it easy to move onto the rest of the blocks.

STEP 1 Starting from a corner of the block, quilt a leaflike shape so that it fills in half the block. *Fig. A*

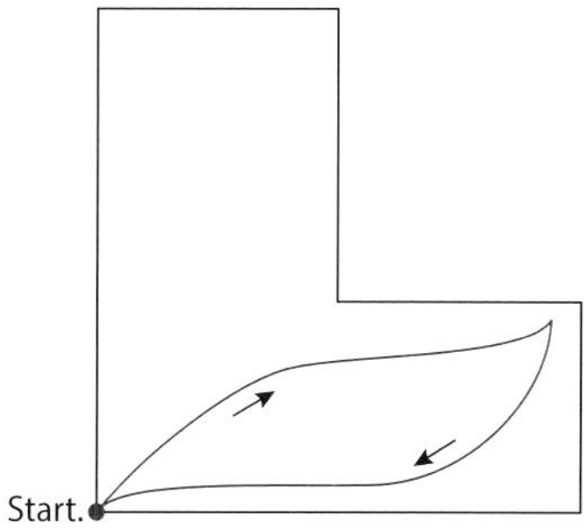

A

STEP 2 Repeat by quilting another leaflike shape in the other half, returning to the starting point. *Fig. B*

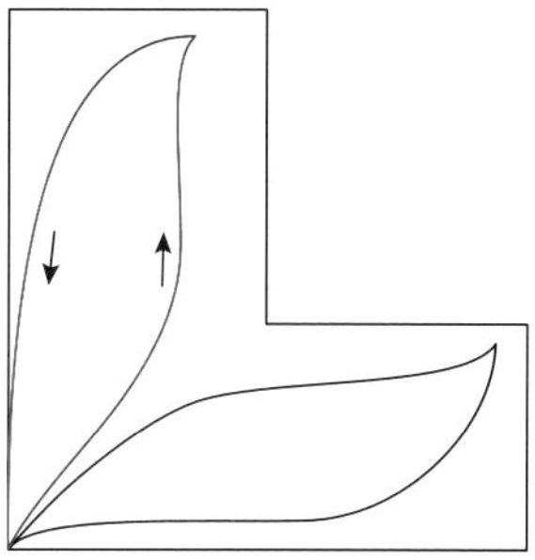

B

Flowered Curves

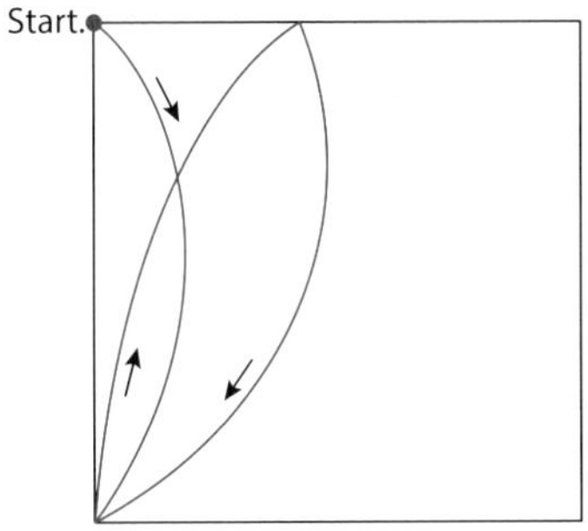

C

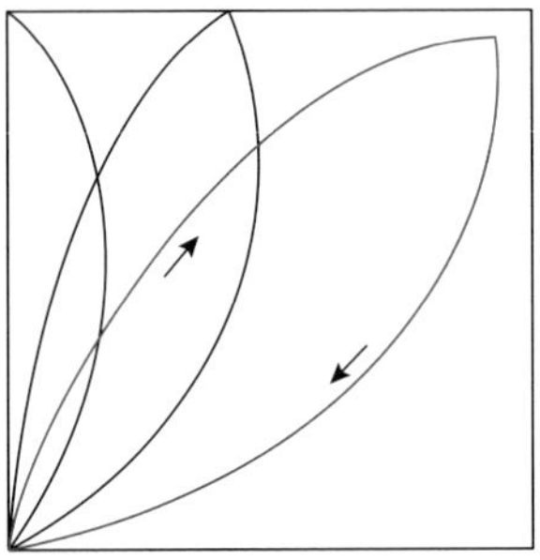

D

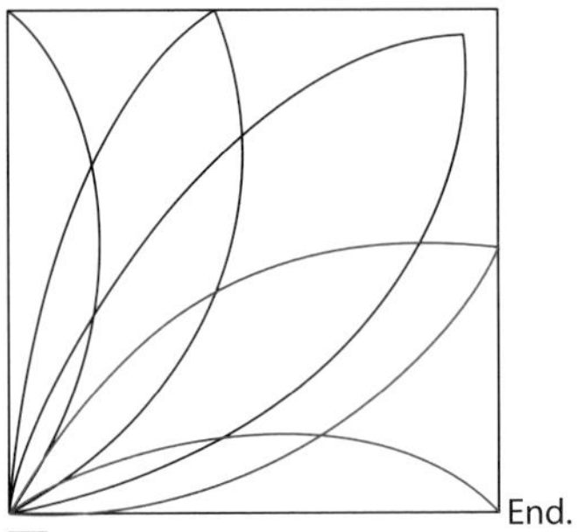

E

Quilt this flowery design pointing away from the center; it will look as though petals are radiating from the center.

STEP 1 Starting from a corner, quilt a line that curves out and to the next corner. This corner will be where most of the curves will return. Quilt another line that curves out to the midpoint of the top side and curves back to the same point. *Fig. C*

STEP 2 Repeat Step 1, curving out to the opposite point and returning. *Fig. D*

STEP 3 Continue quilting the rest of the block until you reach the outside corner of the block. *Fig. E*

THE LAST STEP

Add the binding to your quilt, referring to Binding (page 14) as needed. Note that *Medallion* requires about 330″ of binding.

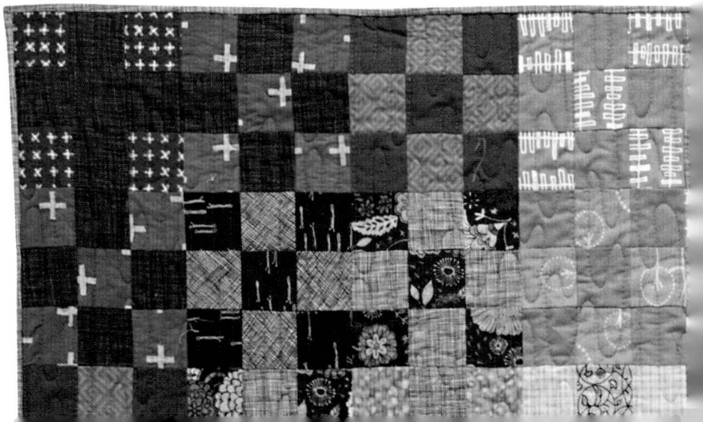

About the Authors

JENIFER DICK began quilting in 1993 when, on a whim, she signed up for a beginning quiltmaking class. From that first stitch, she was hooked. In 2003, she started teaching and lecturing at quilt shops and guilds, and shortly after, published her first book, *Grapefruit Juice and Sugar*.

She is the author of five quilt books and her work has been published in many other books and magazines. Her pattern company, Everyday Stitches (everydaystitches.com), produces quality quilt patterns for all skill levels.

Website:
42quilts.com

Facebook:
/42quilts

Instagram:
@jeniferdick

ALSO BY JENIFER DICK

ANGELA WALTERS is a machine quilter and author who loves to teach others to use quilting to bring out the best in their quilts. Her work has been published in numerous magazines and books. She shares tips and finished quilts on her blog and believes that "quilting is the funnest part!"

Website:
quiltingismytherapy.com

Facebook:
/angelafmq

Pinterest:
/ange_walters1

Instagram:
@angelafmq

ALSO BY ANGELA WALTERS

Want even more creative content?
Go to ctpub.com/offer
& sign up to receive our gift to you!
MENU
C&T PUBLISHING
Your Home for Creative Quilting & Sewing
HAND PRINTING STUDIO
Print on Almost Anything!
Get some in-spiration
GET INSPIRED
GARMENT SEWING LOOKBOOK 2016
58
59
Make it, snap it, share it
using #ctpublishing